Matt Cohen and His Works

Matt Cohen (1942–)

GEORGE WOODCOCK

Biography

MATT COHEN was born at Kingston, Ontario, on 30 December 1942. In early childhood, he moved with his family to Ottawa, and there he attended grade school and high school, from which he graduated in 1960. His parents were Jewish, but, as he has remarked, he was not brought up very religiously. After graduating from high school, he went on to the University of Toronto, where he graduated with a B.A. (honours) in 1964. His postgraduate degree was an M.A. in political theory, gained from the University of Toronto in 1965; the subject of his thesis was the French novelist and political maverick Albert Camus. In 1967 Cohen began his brief academic career as a lecturer in the Department of Religion at McMaster University; he has always been careful to explain that he was not teaching theology, but the sociology of religion. His academic preoccupations have found their places in his writing, for political theory provides the central thematic cord in his futurist novel *The Colours of War*, and religion, observed as a force in society, plays a high role in *Flowers of Darkness*.

In 1968 Cohen abandoned his teaching career to take up full-time writing, though on several occasions since that time he has loosely remade his academic links; he was writer-in-residence at the University of Alberta between 1975 and 1976, Visiting Professor of Creative Writing at the University of Victoria between 1979 and 1980, writer-in-residence at the University of Western Ontario in 1981, and Visiting Professor at the University of Bologna in 1984.

After leaving McMaster, Cohen lived briefly in Toronto and in 1970 retired to write on a farm near Godfrey, in the country north of Kingston. Later he returned for a while to live in Toronto, though rural Ontario has always drawn him back. He was fiction editor at The Coach House Press for a period and prepared the second volume of Coach House's anthology *The Story So Far*, which appeared in

1973. He has lived briefly in the Queen Charlotte Islands off the coast of British Columbia; a Canada Council grant in 1977 took him to England; and, among his other travels, he spent a period in Spain in 1980, after his assignment at the University of Victoria came to an end, collecting material for the novel that eventually became *The Spanish Doctor.* More recently, he has spent a period in Paris (1985) gathering material for a yet uncompleted novel.

Cohen has worked in a variety of genres. He has written a radio play and two television plays; he has done sporadic book reviewing; there is the ironic poetry of *Peach Melba* (1974); and there are the children's fantasies *Too Bad Galahad* (1972) and *The Leaves of Louise* (1978). But principally he is known as a writer of fiction, and this has been his real literary vocation.

His first novel, *Korsoniloff*, appeared in 1969, and this story of a schizophrenic teacher of philosophy derived a great deal from the author's experience of university life. But Cohen's later works show him as a mainly inventive writer, rather than one who derives his material from direct experience. They began with the fantasy novella *Johnny Crackle Sings*, which appeared in 1971. Then, after writing an unsuccessful novel with a linear chronology, which he abandoned unpublished, Cohen went on to the series of substantial novels, less overtly experimental than his first books yet based largely on the manipulation of time flows, that began with the publication of *The Disinherited* in 1974, and carried on with surprisingly regular intervals through *Wooden Hunters* (1975), *The Colours of War* (1977), *The Sweet Second Summer of Kitty Malone* (1979), *Flowers of Darkness* (1981), and *The Spanish Doctor* (1984).

All these novels — except for *Wooden Hunters*, which is set in the Queen Charlotte Islands, and *The Spanish Doctor*, which is set in fifteenth-century Europe — take place in the country north of Kingston where Cohen has spent so much of his time in recent years. It was on his farm there that he wrote the first of his country stories — "Country Music" — and he told the author of the present essay that ". . . it and especially material that was rejected from it became the basis for *The Disinherited* and *The Sweet Second Summer of Kitty Malone*."[1] Several of his stories, as well as the four rural Ontario novels, are centred around an imaginary town named Salem. "*Flowers of Darkness* is the fourth of the Salem novels," Cohen remarked in the same letter, "and I like to think it will be the last."

Cohen's short stories have been published widely in Canadian magazines and have been collected in four volumes: *Columbus and the Fat Lady and Other Stories* (1972), *Night Flights: Stories New and Selected* (1978), *The Expatriate: Collected Short Stories* (1982), and *Café Le Dog* (1983).

At the time of writing, Matt Cohen lives as much as he can on his 170 acres of rocky farmland at Verona, north of Kingston, with intervals in Toronto.

"For some people the right thing to do is to leave home and go somewhere else," Cohen said in a 1981 interview with Alan Twigg. "It's almost inevitable for them. For other people it's almost inevitable to go away and come back. I think I understand those people who come back better than those who go away."[2]

In the same interview, he also said, ". . . I think I could quit writing quite soon" (Twigg, p. 184).

Tradition and Milieu

Until the 1960s, comparatively little experimental fiction was being written in Canada. Poetry had already moved forward, propelled by a series of avant-gardes; but novelists, even though they had begun to interpret the national myths, were doing so in largely traditional ways. Morley Callaghan — perhaps our first experimental novelist — had fitted into the American pattern of the 1930s rather than into any Canadian movement towards a new kind of novel, and writers like Howard O'Hagan and Sheila Watson with their mythical fantasies were exceptional in their times, the end of the 1930s and the 1950s respectively. Apart from the formula fiction represented most notably by Mazo de la Roche's Jalna romances, the prevalent mode was a modified realism. Among Prairie writers — notably Frederick Philip Grove, that resurrected German littérateur — this mode perpetuated some of the elements of European naturalism. The most important of Eastern Canadian quasi realists, up to the 1950s, was Hugh MacLennan, a classical scholar obsessed by the *Odyssey*, and in his case the realism was diluted not only by remembered mythology but also by a didactic outlook, so that his novels tended to read like fictional essays, each proving a point about the destiny of Canada. Even a writer like Margaret Laurence, who emerged in the early 1960s, combined a descriptive realism with the urge, which united her with younger writers, to liberate her forms by manipulating time and memory and so breaking the lockgrip of chronological linearity.

Canadian fiction really began to follow poetry into modernity towards the end of the 1960s. Leonard Cohen's *Beautiful Losers* appeared in 1966, Marian Engel's *No Clouds of Glory*, in 1968, and – all in the one year of 1969 – Margaret Atwood's first novel, *The Edible Woman*, Robert Kroetsch's ambitious and innovative third novel, *The Studhorse Man*, and Matt Cohen's first and very experimental novella, *Korsoniloff*.

Each in its own way, these books were all events in the transformation of the Canadian novel. It was not an abrupt abandonment of traditional forms, for writers like Marian Engel, Margaret Atwood, and Matt Cohen have been easy in adopting the forms most suitable to their immediate needs, and these have sometimes been at least neo-traditional. But the 1960s, and especially the last years of that decade, represent a maturing of the novel as a literary form that has enabled it to open out from the constrictions inevitable in a closed-in, pioneer culture and has freed writers to move between multiple formal options. In maturing, a literature not only becomes liberated, so that it has its own identity even when it maintains its links with older cultures, but it also, by that very token, assumes a power of variegation. Writers become less constrained by formula, less dominated by didactic imperatives, and therefore less predictable and more sharply individual.

It is into this pattern that Matt Cohen fits. He is the contemporary of a whole group of young Canadian writers who have emerged into public and critical attention since the end of the 1960s, and his personal links and artistic affinities with many of them have been close. Yet what struck many perceptive readers about Cohen's first book, the novella *Korsoniloff*, was that its analogues, and perhaps the works that had most influenced it, could be found more easily in European than in North American fiction. There is a sharp and ironic edge to it that reminds one of Gide's novellas, and a haunting echo of Kafka in the central character's failure to establish which of his warring personae is the real one. In its combination of psychological density and intellectual translucency, *Korsoniloff* resembles the works of French *nouvelle vague* novelists of the preceding decade like Marguerite Duras and Nathalie Sarraute, more than it does anything written in Canada up to its time.

It is also impossible to forget, when one reads the whole corpus of Cohen's fiction, that during his university period the subject of his thesis was the political thought of Albert Camus. In Camus it is more difficult to separate the politics from the art than it is with a less integrated novelist like Jean-Paul Sartre. And it is when Cohen introduces a political element into his work, as in *The Colours of War*, where he enters deeply into the morality of rebellion, that one realizes how much he has learned from Camus in the ability to subsume the didactic argument into the fictional structure of an essentially philosophic novel. Korsoniloff is certainly, in his own way, a Camusian "stranger," and the sense of the absurd that so permeates the French writer's novels, like *L'Etranger* and *La Peste*, is strongly present in Cohen's novels, and notably in *Wooden Hunters*, with its poignant juxtapositions of human violence and natural beauty. The "benign indifference of the universe" — that concept so central to an understanding of Camus — hovers over all of Cohen's novels, with their extreme sensitivity to the cruel beauty of nature; and the kind of assertion of human dignity in the face of the absurd that is the very essence of a novel like *La Peste* lies also at the Ontarian heart of *The Sweet Second Summer of Kitty Malone*.

Writers choose their influences, if these are productive, because of their affinities. But affinities, when they are stated, can often define a writer's aims or even his sense of himself. Cohen has long admired Orwell, yet it is less easy to suggest that he was influenced by him as he clearly was by Albert Camus, even though there are evident similarities, at certain points, between his futurist novel, *The Colours of War*, and *Nineteen Eighty-Four.* But beyond the area of subject, a great deal is suggested by one of Cohen's remarks in a letter to the author of this essay:

> What is so attractive to me, about George Orwell — or Margaret Laurence at her best — is that the voice is both simple and flexible, and yet so natural that one feels that this is not simply a voice produced by craft, but is actually a voice that necessarily springs from the person.

Such a sentence gives one a glancing view of Orwell and Laurence, tells one a little more about the affinities that Cohen recognizes and accepts, but tells one most about Cohen's own intent as a prose writer. If we juxtapose his phrase "a voice that necessarily springs from the person" with Orwell's "prose . . . like a window pane,"[3] we learn a great deal, not only about the two writers, but also about their relationship.

In Canadian terms, Cohen emerged at the end of the 1960s as a contributor to one of the remarkable phenomena of recent Canadian writing, the emergence of a group of young experimental fiction writers at the very time when other writers were establishing the experimental small presses which would produce their work. *Korsoniloff*, and Cohen's first book of stories, *Columbus and the Fat Lady*, were both issued by the House of Anansi, which was founded by two young writers, Dave Godfrey and Dennis Lee, and which began publication in 1967; later, Margaret Atwood, Graeme Gibson, Shirley Gibson, and other writers were closely involved in operating Anansi. The third of Cohen's early books, *Too Bad Galahad* (1972), was published by The Coach House Press, another small, experimental house run by writers, in which Cohen himself became involved as an editor. *Korsoniloff* appeared in Spiderline Editions, a series of experimental fiction conceived by Dennis Lee and devoted entirely to "first novels." For a couple of years, the series tapped unexploited sources of imaginative energy, but then the flow of brilliant available material dried up and the series expired.

Among the novels published in Spiderline Editions were Peter Such's *Fallout*, John Sandman's *Eating Out*, Russell Marois's *The Telephone Pole*, Michael Charters' *Victor Victim*, and Rachel Wyatt's *The String Box*. All these novels were idiosyncratic and experimental, some to the point of obscurity, and they represented — as did Margaret Atwood's *The Edible Woman* and Marian Engel's early novels of about the same time — the emergence of a new generation of fiction writers. These were the Canadian writers with whom, when he first emerged, Cohen had the closest affinities. Some of them became his friends, but to judge how far any of them influenced him, except by the sharing of views and attitudes and perhaps by a degree of mutual criticism, is problematical, since he was so clearly already the most accomplished of the Spiderliners. When he unexpectedly turned to a melodramatic, generational epic in his first full-length novel, *The Disinherited*, the influence of no other Canadian writer was evident.

Indeed, as Cohen moved into his larger novels, the resemblances that appeared have been less to other Canadian writers than to American novelists, and especially to Southern novelists like William Faulkner and Erskine Caldwell. In part, admittedly, the resemblance has been due to the choice of similar terrains, for the decaying farms of the once-prosperous Ontario countryside, and their violent inhabitants whom city people regard as degenerate, have much in common with decaying farms and their people in the deep South, and small, inbred towns like Salem are standbys of Southern fiction. While Cohen also resembles Faulkner in his creation of a special country for his fiction, built equally out of memory and imagination, the destructive combination of religion, lust, and violence in *Flowers of Darkness* is a pattern that has many analogues in Southern novels. Perhaps Cohen is not influenced to the extent of actual imitation by writers like Faulkner and Caldwell, yet he obviously finds in them deep affinities and has been able to use some of their fictional inventions for his own purposes, and not always without the intent of parody.

Critical Overview and Context

Though Matt Cohen's larger novels and his second book of stories, *Night Flights*, have been extensively reviewed, there have so far been few long and intensive studies of his work. They are in fact confined to the introductions by John Moss to the New Canadian Library editions of *The Disinherited* and *Wooden Hunters*, and my own essay "Armies Moving in the Night: The Fictions of Matt Cohen," which appeared during 1979 in the *International Fiction Review* and was afterwards lengthened and included in my *The World of Canadian Writing: Critiques and Recollections* (1980); since the main arguments in that paper surface in the fourth section of the present essay, there is no need to summarize them. There are also brief essays on Cohen's work by Norah Story in the *Supplement to the Oxford Companion to Canadian History and Literature* (1973) and by Frank Davey in his *From There to Here: A Guide to English-Canadian Literature since 1960* (1974). Graeme Gibson published an interview with Cohen in his *Eleven Canadian Novelists* (1973), and Alan Twigg included another in *For Openers* (1981).

Reviews of Cohen's early books were few and wavered between the extremes of praise and blame that a young, experimental writer customarily encounters. Wayne R. Smith in the *The Citizen* [Ottawa] termed *Johnny Crackle Sings* an "abortion, . . . the hackneyed effort of an incompetent author";[4] Doug Austen in the counter-cultural *Guerilla* called it "a masterpiece";[5] Donald Cameron in *Maclean's* temperately remarked that ". . . it chimes with experience, with what one hears on the streets and the jukeboxes";[6] and Jack Batten in *The Globe Magazine* related it to the realities of the "fragmented . . . rock world" and praised Cohen for "getting such an elusive thing into print so honestly."[7] Cohen's first book of stories, *Columbus and the Fat Lady*, was saluted by Douglas Barbour for the excellence of its "speculative fiction,"[8] and Robert Harlow remarked that Cohen "knows that the short story is a way of stopping life so that it can happen, and that out of this paradox rises form."[9]

As soon as Cohen published a full-length novel — *The Disinherited* — with a leading publisher (McClelland and Stewart), the reviews became more numerous, though still extremely varied in their verdicts. Wilma Breakwell in *The Owen Sound Sun-Times* found it "dank, drab, dreary and dirty" with "utter chaos in its continuity."[10] David Watmough, speaking on CBC Radio, granted that Cohen's "characters as well as his Ontario landscape all suggest the instinctive confidence of the born writer" yet found a "sense of staleness" in the rural theme.[11] David McFadden identified the novel as "old-fashioned, traditional, naturalistic, psychological" yet so "experimental" in its multiplication of levels that the dedicated reader would find "his way of looking at rural life in Ontario forever altered."[12] Jack Batten noted the masterly handling of time: "Present flows into memory, past merges with reality, sometimes events in two separate generations run together in the same sentence, and all of it happens in ways that have two truths, logical and poetic."[13] Patricia Morley found analogues to *The Disinherited* in "Beckett and the Theatre of the Absurd" and summed up: "This is black comedy, but still comic, with all the hope and courage that comedy implies."[14] Like many other reviewers, Roy MacSkimming heard echoes of Faulkner, yet concluded that ". . . the literary influence has been absorbed and Cohen knows his rural Ontario Protestants, their history and psychology and speech, too well to be derivative in any fundamental way."[15] In a long, thoughtful review in *The Fiddlehead*, Anthony Brennan found Cohen's attempts to link past and present "too pat . . . , too intrusive, too strenuously enforced." Yet he admitted the ambitious scope of the novel and concluded: "In the descriptions of the texture of relations between men and women, the ebb and flow of jealousy, tenderness, violence, love, in the way he convinces us of the emotional mapping which one generation imposes on the next he has produced a compelling story which makes one look forward eagerly to his next work."[16] Finally, in his Introduction to the New Canadian Library edition of *The Disinherited*, John Moss remarked on the way "irony permeates the whole, for what is shown in process is also shown to end. Whatever enters time is also lost in time." Yet, unlike the reviewers who found only negation in the novel, Moss regarded it as "an evocative celebration of the wholeness of life" projecting "the view of reality which necessarily includes the horror with the glory, where life and death coexist in a divine comedy on a secular plane."[17]

Many reviewers found *Wooden Hunters* inferior to *The Disinherited*. John Mills in *The Fiddlehead* thought that "the sombre style, so effective in *The Disinherited*, here becomes merely portentous," and that Cohen's narrative skills were wasted because ". . . the vacuity of plot and character turns them into self-indulgent mannerisms."[18] Paul Stuewe in *Books in Canada* found Cohen relying on "trite expressions that avoid the novelist's responsibility to show as well as tell."[19] Francis Mansbridge in the *Canadian Fiction Magazine* thought that the novel was satisfyingly complex but that ". . . the cool, detached tone . . . inhibits the full realization of characters and events. Cohen is not a good observer of realistic detail."[20] George Russell found the "meaningless groping" by which the characters try to reach each other "morbid and paralyzing." Cohen he described as "an earnest and skillful writer" with "an excellent eye for the minutiae of his claustrophobic world" who "never probes very deeply, because to do so would force him to abandon his deadpan pose."[21] John Ayre complained about the "violence and eruptions" and saw *Wooden Hunters* as an "Atwoodian encyclopaedia of bludgeoned victims," people whose effort to find themselves "seems only to have left them in a soulless chaos where good and evil have ceased to have meaning." He found the novel "ultimately indulgent and unsatisfying."[22]

Roy MacSkimming, on the other hand, while granting that *Wooden Hunters* is "a smaller book, both literally and figuratively," than *The Disinherited*, saw Matt Cohen as "a novelist with a rare gift" who "takes us inside his characters as few writers can and renders them, in a finely pitched prose, exactly and vividly on their own terms, rather than using them as symbolic vehicles or social types." Cohen does this "not with explanatory monologues or tedious psychologizing, but by making a physical universe of each character. He begins and ends with the body and the senses. It's an approach that makes his people impossible to forget."[23] And Jack Batten, one of the few reviewers to claim that *Wooden Hunters* was better than *The Disinherited*, praised Cohen's ability to get "inside his people's heads" and his "great talent for detail — for filling in the colours and the feel and spirit of things."[24]

Reviewers' reactions to *The Colours of War* were similarly mixed, largely because many of them took literally its political content and failed to understand the fabulist intent that puts it into the category of *Gulliver's Travels* or *Candide* rather than into that of *L'Espoir* or *Darkness at Noon*. In an exceptionally malicious review in *The Globe and Mail*, Norman Snider blamed Cohen because his "political sentiment is 10 years old";[25] and Tom Middlebro' in *The Citizen* [Ottawa] suggested that Cohen's vision had come from the 1960s and, on the assumption that this was a political novel, criticized the fact that ". . . Matt Cohen's hero makes no effort to understand and evaluate the rival forces . . . ."[26] A similar criticism — polemical rather than literary in its direction — was made by Peter Stevens when he said that ". . . the novel remains flawed because the revolutionary fervour and social upheaval are too generally conceived. And, while [Theodore's] personal working out of his life is well presented, he still remains elusive in terms of his connections with the revolution and social commitment."[27] A more balanced view was that of Ken Adachi, who recognized that, if one were to think in literal terms, ". . . Cohen thrusts his character into a set of symbolic incidents that severely tests the reader's willing suspension of disbelief," but who also saw that Cohen's prose had, "if anything, . . . become leaner, sharper, more economical." Furthermore, Adachi recognized the importance of the last third of the book — the Salem section — where ". . . Theodore is able to kill out of love, just as he previously was unable to kill for the revolution."[28]

Perhaps because of its more positive sentiments, *The Sweet Second Summer of Kitty Malone* fared better with the reviewers than any of Cohen's books since *The Disinherited*. Timothy Findley remarked that "dreams are part and parcel of every life. But Cohen seizes on this fact to give a mythic edge to his story and its characters . . . . It is our dreams that refine our individuality. And it is their dreams that give stature, beauty and clarity to the people in this book." He hailed *The Sweet Second Summer* as "wonderful proof that talent cannot be silenced by time."[29] Gerald Noonan spoke of the book as a "triumphant affirmation of Matt Cohen's maturity as a novelist" and claimed that ". . . Cohen's novel transcends the terrain of Ontario's rural east and illuminates the real and the irrational in the human mind. Upon a layer of thin soil, each generation confronts its morality, as well as the false promise of hard work, cheap rye and the relief of sex and violence."[30] Patricia Morley registered a mild dissent from the general praise, finding areas of overwriting in *The Sweet Second Summer* – "overblown prose with a frenzied, hectic air that falls into bathos" – and ranking it as second to *The Disinherited*.[31] Barbara Amiel, having acerbically remarked that ". . . turning the pages becomes an obligation rather than a pleasure," was finally forced to admit that ". . . there is a quality in [Cohen's] writing, a haunting sense of glimpsing the essential beyond the haze of crafted words, that makes the reader go back to the book again and again with the uneasy feeling of having missed something."[32]

Night Flights, Cohen's second book of stories, received a great deal more attention than *Columbus and the Fat Lady*, though in its contents it largely repeated that earlier book. All the reviewers remarked on the variety of approaches. Some, like Michael Thorpe in *Books in Canada*, attempted to isolate what was common to all of them:

> Cohen's style is highly polished. His openings deftly establish setting, atmosphere or central situation, often through a symbolic gesture or an action that serves as a pointer toward the core of significance the reader must seek out. His transitions can be abrupt, but they are not arbitrary and sustain a swift, clean movement. Where his intelligence rather than his sympathy is uppermost, the effect can be slick; in the more memorable stories – at half the collection, an unusually high count – the control and irony are the servants of a compassionate intelligence.[33]

Jon Kertzer in *The Canadian Forum* argued that the more surrealistic stories were the less successful, lacking "the depth which . . . is really the product of style, not of 'deep' thoughts"; recognizing the importance of the country stories that led to *The Disinherited* and *The Sweet Second Summer*, he remarked:

> The Frank brothers, who appear in only three stories, dominate the book. They are the most compelling characters, the most disorderly, disreputable and violent . . . . The Frank brothers arouse our distaste, yet also our sympathy and even affection because they feel their losses — of youth, vigour, love, dignity — most intensely even though they are the least articulate people in the book.[34]

A rare American review, by Gary T. Davenport in *The Sewanee Review*, was interesting for comments that came from outside the Canadian literary world, yet which largely confirmed the views expressed by the better Canadian critics:

> Cohen's chief thematic concerns are time and the nature of reality, and his style is often intentionally repetitive and cyclical — as in "Columbus and the Fat Lady," in which he effectively creates the impression that the events of the story have neither beginning nor end. The reader frequently finds himself asking whether something is *really* happening or is only the delirium of this or that character's distorted mind. (And Cohen has depicted his share of distorted minds.) Of course the narrative technique treads a thin line here, and it is sometimes uncertain, sometimes masterful. The author's control of language is one of the most gratifying features of his work.[35]

Generally speaking, *Flowers of Darkness* was well received by the critics, several of whom noted how well Cohen had controlled the potentially melodramatic features of the novel, which Ken Adachi described as "those alarming elements we associate with soap operas or cheap commercial fiction: murder, lust, suicide, erotic sex, blackmail, jealousy and hate." Cohen, Adachi suggested, can write his way out of the negative potentialities of such fiction because "his prose is flowing, elegiac and supple, and there is nothing soggy about it . . . . He is not simply an entertainer. He has a view, and a merciless view it often is, not only of rural life but of its social attitudes . . . ." Cohen has the power of probing deeply into human feelings and can, "apparently without effort, make the reader feel the sadness of disillusionment, the vanity of vain regret. And the throb of guilt . . . can be felt like a toothache."[36] Douglas Hamilton saw a more didactic purpose at work in *Flowers of Darkness*: "With hyperbole and biting irony, Cohen mocks the hegemony that the Protestant church exercises over the souls of rural Ontario and ridicules the bogus piety of many Christian fundamentalists."[37]

Wayne Grady viewed *Flowers of Darkness* as the culmination of a "steady and purposeful" progress and noted that if Cohen "sometimes picks up threads and characters and leaves them undeveloped, there is no doubt that his themes are important and his inspiration genuine." Nevertheless Grady saw the *deus ex machina* ominously at work in *Flowers of Darkness*: ". . . it does seem at times that an abstract and impersonal fate moves the stock characters in Cohen's morality play."[38] In my own review, I noted the element of melodrama in the novel and remarked that "actuality is never quite like this." I went on to ask:

> But is the actual always the real? That, perhaps, is the great question the art of fiction is always set to pose. And the answer lies, surely, in how far we become willing hostages in the country of the mind a novel creates . . . . For it is the consistency of the imaginative construct, rather than the likeness to anything in what we oddly call "real life," that we in fact seek in fiction. And that kind of consistency, it seems to me, Matt Cohen has achieved.[39]

As Ken Adachi also did, Paul Stuewe noted that ". . . one of the most enjoyable aspects of *Flowers of Darkness* is the assurance with which Matt Cohen sketches his secondary characters and the physical setting of Salem." He went on:

> There's a fine line between excessive realism, which tells us more than we want to know, and insufficient realism, which makes it difficult for us to feel a part of fictional creation, and I think that here Cohen has hit it just about right. He leaves no doubt in our minds about the reality of Salem and its citizens, but we're also encouraged to use our imaginations in filling in some of the ambiguities which the author wisely refuses to resolve.

Stuewe remarked that the one serious failing of *Flowers of Darkness*, "typical of much of Cohen's work, is the usage of clichéd, awkward or even downright purple prose when he describes a particularly charged emotional experience." He found these "sudden outbursts of infelicity" very puzzling, "since [Cohen] is also capable of engrossing us for long stretches of near-flawless writing," and concluded that ". . . this consistent and debilitating attribute keeps his work from fulfilling all its evident promise."[40] In a disappointingly shallow review, Aritha van Herk described Cohen as a "Hawthornesque catechizer" and claimed that "Salem lives in every one of us."[41]

The reaction of critics to *Café Le Dog* was largely one of disappointment. Some felt uneasy about the whole book; others praised some stories at the expense of the rest; few were wholly satisfied. The sense of a negation more lifeless, more nihilistic, than that which sometimes appears in the Salem novels was expressed by some critics. Anthony Bukoski recalled Gogol's classic of black humour when he entitled his review "Dead Souls" and expanded the thought: ". . . Cohen's dead souls fear history — both the relatively recent past of their own wrecked lives and their antecedents' longer, deeper history, which sometimes goes back as far as the Spanish Inquisition." Though he saw here and there a reaffirmation of life, Bukoski remarked in conclusion: "Usually sombre of tone, the eight stories here are sometimes frightening; they offer so bleak a world-view." Yet he admitted that Cohen often presents his "bleak world-view" with literary skill. "There is fine writing here nonetheless. Cohen's often leisurely exposition, especially in the long first story, accretes details that later return to haunt reader and character alike."[42] George Galt balanced Gogol with Eliot at his most negative when he called his review "The Hollow Men." He saw Cohen regressing in *Café Le Dog* towards the preoccupations of his earlier works like *Korsoniloff*, moving back into a "rootless urban world where characters have little control over their lives . . . . Hollow men, they appear to be imitating life's form without embracing its content." He made an exception for two stories, "The Sins of Tomas Benares" and "Sentimental Meetings" (both about Spanish Jews and anticipatory of *The Spanish Doctor*), and remarked that the characters in them "are developed with insight and tenderness." But he found the book on the whole "not impressive." Cohen "appears to be toying with new directions in this book, but much of it suffers from diminished intensity and even flippancy when compared to earlier work . . . ."[43]

Ken Adachi also picked out "The Sins of Tomas Benares" for special praise, but his general judgement of *Café Le Dog* was unflattering. Most of the pieces, he claimed, "are hardly stories at all but function as anecdotes, thin magazine-ish stuff lacking subtlety. This would not matter if we did not know that Cohen is a writer of considerable proven talent, who has written books more humanly useful and interesting."[44] William French was somewhat more positive, seeing *Café Le Dog* as a demonstration of Cohen's "remarkable versatility, both in style and subject matter." But even he, picking the two longest stories as the best, expressed the view that ". . . Cohen is a better novelist than a short-story writer" and complained of the "oddly unsatisfying" quality of the two stories in the book that depart from realism ("At the Empress Hotel" and "Café Le Dog"). He suggested we contain our disappointment by regarding *Café Le Dog* as "a progress report on [Cohen's] career rather than a self-sustaining work."[45] Jon Kertzer, in one of the few really positive reviews of *Café Le Dog*, described the field of perception the book reveals and praised its modest virtues, noting the special strategy of these stories: they "begin with deceptive simplicity and end inconclusively, but in the middle prove psychologically complex." With a shrewd and obliquely correct insight, Kertzer remarked that the stories about Tomas Benares and his son "read like chapters from a novel, and it will be interesting to see if Cohen, who tends to get possessed by his characters, will present them in future work."[46] Cohen in fact would not incorporate either Benares in a longer fiction, but his next novel was indeed to be about another Spanish doctor who came, four centuries before, from the same city of Toledo as the Benares clan.

The Spanish Doctor provoked more division among Cohen's critics than any other of his books. I spoke well of it in terms very similar to my treatment in the present essay, and Marian Engel, though she was never able to review the book, spoke to me of its imaginative power. Mark Abley regarded it as an audacious book and Cohen's hero, Avram Halevi, as "one of the strongest characters [Cohen] has ever created." But he noted the unevenness of the prose, whose "finest moments are those in which Cohen's own feelings exert the greatest pressure on his writing — notably his furious, plaintive descriptions of the doomed Jews of Spain"; at other times, the prose becomes "limp and lazy," and Abley noted, as some other readers have done, that there are "some extensive descriptions of sex and violence which are not necessary to the plot."[47]

Alberto Manguel approached the book as a good story in the tradition of Rider Haggard: ". . . its soul is in its matter, not in its character or its form." The plot, he declared, "is certainly gripping," but in comparison the characters, even Avram, "seem less vivid." Moreover, in Manguel's view, the book "must be read almost in spite of the language. The images have the uneasy look of fake antiques . . . ." He concluded: "Matt Cohen has decided to tell a story, and the story works. It has the excitement of Sunday afternoon movies, like much of *Macbeth*, and the sweep of historical sagas, like those of Victor Hugo. It is a book whose pages demand to be turned, and that alone, in a wilderness of boring bestsellers, is of no little merit."[48]

That is praise, even if somewhat backhanded, but the very qualities Manguel saw as virtues have been used by other critics to condemn Cohen. Norman Sigurdson dismissed the book as "really nothing more than an improbable melodrama chock-full of sex and violence and dressed up in medieval garb. It owes more to Harold Robbins than to Isaac Bashevis Singer."[49] Ken Adachi, on the whole a critic friendly to Cohen, came to similar conclusions. He granted that the novel is "a grandly, almost quixotically ambitious project" and that in struggling with it Cohen "achieves moments of moral passion" and that he offers "pungent and plentiful" vignettes of mediaeval Europe. What Adachi found disappointing is that ". . . this weighty and uncomfortable subject is floated in gallons of melodrama and schmaltz. By turns *Fiddler on the Roof* and a romance novel, it drags its way to an affectedly sentimental conclusion." The final turn of Adachi's screw came when he recalled "The Sins of Tomas Benares" in *Café Le Dog* and remarked: "That story, within a few economical pages, imparted more lasting force than is found in this novel."[50]

Frank Davey found more to praise in *The Spanish Doctor*. He noted that it is an "overwhelmingly physical book" and approved its fastidious attention "to texture, weight, surface, smell, taste, touch," its loving evocation of the surface of life. But he claimed that "the moral action of the book" does not sustain this vision and that the characterization fails because Cohen does not reveal enough of the inner life of his people "to demonstrate that they must necessarily become puppets, or that their yielding to physical exigency is anything more than the banal choice of the stereotypical character." He saw *The Spanish Doctor* as the "penultimate draft" of a historical novel "remarkable in its intellectual grasp of human dilemma, remarkable in its evocation of the erotic texture of medieval surface," but lacking the very "narrative strategy" in which Cohen's earlier novels had excelled.[51]

Cohen's Works

Matt Cohen might be described as a high realist pursuing a course remarkably analogous to that of some of the more vital contemporary Canadian visual artists. There are times in the history of the arts when the preoccupations of writers and painters seem far apart and it is difficult to make any comparisons between them. But at other times, one can find echoes and reflections which point to a unity of consciousness among the arts that, in terms of the senses through which they work, are entirely different. For literature, though the eyes read it on the page, is really codified sound, and visual only in so far as it sets out to evoke images in the mind's eye.

Yet the matter of the mind's eye is important, for, to go a little further, the times when one senses a unity embracing the pictorial and the literary arts are those periods when literature is especially visual in its creation of images and therefore little inclined to resort to abstract verbalization, while the visual arts have also turned away from abstraction and extreme formalism to assume a role of quasi-poetic suggestiveness linked to a high degree of figurative representation.

Such times are often interesting and vital culturally: consider the great period in France, between the revolution of 1848 and the Commune of 1870, when the poet Baudelaire wrote so understandingly on the melodramatic paintings of Delacroix. His understanding mirrored a pattern of *correspondances* — to use his own word — that linked the multichromatic orientalist visions of Delacroix's paintings with the more exotic poems of *Les Fleurs du mal* and, one step removed, with the illuminated realism of Flaubert's rendering of a half-known past, *Salammbô*. Tonally, these works echo one to the other; the harmony is rarely false.

In Canada today, we seem to be going through a similar period. Many of the most interesting painters — Alex Colville, Christopher

Pratt, Ivan Eyre, Tom Forrestal, the late Jack Chambers — have been working through various forms of high realism, in which the technique is mimetic — a quasi-photographic representation of actuality — but the tone is heightened to that of magic illumination, and the images are arranged in combinations impossible in real life. Since few — if any — of these artists depend on dreams to provide their subject matter, one cannot identify their work with surrealism, which was a historical movement with limited aims. But certainly Herbert Read's wider term *superrealism*, suggesting a magnified awareness of reality, could be used to describe them.

At the same time, and in a very similar way, many Canadian novelists have been combining a heightened verisimilitude in description, which presents the physical world with preternatural clarity, with a tendency to create larger-than-life figures caught in situations that resemble those of myth rather than those of real life. One finds such larger-than-life figures appearing as early as Howard O'Hagan's *Tay John* in 1939, and repeated later in the characters of Sheila Watson's *The Double Hook*, in the grotesques of Mordecai Richler's *Cocksure* and Margaret Atwood's *Lady Oracle*, in the synthetic beings of Leonard Cohen's *Beautiful Losers*, and in the exuberant, hollow men of Robert Kroetsch's novels. But the placing of this kind of figure in a setting of high realism has perhaps best been done by Matt Cohen in his novels and stories of the rural hinterland of Kingston, centred largely on the little stone town of Salem.

In all, up to the present, there are fourteen volumes of Cohen's fiction. Two of them, *Korsoniloff* and *Johnny Crackle Sings*, are experimental, the products of the author's tentative twenties. *Too Bad Galahad* and *The Leaves of Louise* are written for children. *Night Flights*, the second collection of short stories, largely repeats the contents of its predecessor, *Columbus and the Fat Lady*, though it contains several new items. *The Expatriate* contains all the stories from the first two collections, as well as the previously unpublished title piece, while *Café Le Dog* consists wholly of uncollected pieces. All the remaining six fictions are full-length novels and are largely in the traditional mode, the strangeness of their plots and people masked, as in Swift, by the verisimilitude of description that makes easy our suspension of disbelief. *The Disinherited* hides its profound reflections on the mortality of human societies, and on the way time becomes objectified in life, under the form of a family chronicle. *Wooden Hunters* is an elegy on dying peoples and cultures, but it is also a study of the play of sex and violence in a society where all the traditional restraints, external and internal, have vanished. *The Colours of War* is a political fantasy in which the search for the future becomes, in the end, a flight into the past. *The Sweet Second Summer of Kitty Malone* is a violent and tender study of love surviving age and degeneration. In *Flowers of Darkness*, with the perfect stone facades of the imaginary town of Salem as backdrop, a drama of sin and retribution is acted out, with destiny arranged as inexorably as it ever was in the plays of Aeschylus and Sophocles. And in *The Spanish Doctor*, a complex historical novel, Cohen departs from the twentieth century and rural Ontario to offer a tale of adventure and moral conflict played out over fifteenth-century Europe from Toledo to Kiev.

The five novels set in Canada represent the heart of Cohen's achievement, and we may perhaps take them as pointing the direction of his writing from this middle point of his career, through the creation of the imaginary landscape of Salem which he has made especially his own, much as Faulkner did Yoknapatawpha County and Hardy did Dorset. Yet the two novellas and the short stories give first expression to Cohen's lasting formal and thematic preoccupations and largely establish his language.

One does not know whether there is any special significance for the author in the fact that *Columbus and the Fat Lady* and *Night Flights* both contain fifteen stories. Perhaps more important, as an indication of Cohen's own sense of the direction of his search for the satisfactory form, is that, out of the fifteen stories that appeared in *Columbus and the Fat Lady* in 1972, only four found their way, in 1978, into the "Stories New and Selected," and one of those, "The Toy Pilgrim," was considerably changed. But in even the rejected stories one can see elements that become important in Cohen's novels beginning to emerge: the continual juxtaposition of the literal and the fantastic; the relativity of time to perception; the solitude that is inescapable in the most social of settings. There are passages of dialogue as cross-purposed as anything in Chekhov, and as potent in revealing the failure of human understanding in people who lead lives without direction. Such people are bound by obsessions, prisoners, not merely of the great confining factors of passion and death, but also of the pettiest circumstances of their lives, and because they have not been able to liberate their actions, they cannot realize their potentialities or create themselves as a free individual might. The student of Camus is much present in such stories as "The Watchmaker," "Spadina Time," and "The Nurse from Outer Space," and perhaps their naked existentialism is one of the reasons why they were left out of the later collection.

Night Flights is a much more varied book than *Columbus and the Fat Lady*, mainly because it covers a longer period and is more strictly selected to avoid monotony. Indeed, there is no book in which Cohen's technical virtuosity and versatility are better displayed, though to appreciate the scope of his fictional vision and the depth of his empathy for human predicaments, one has to turn to the novels. The stories vary in tone and approach, from the mannered and decadent fantasy of "The Cure" and "A Literary History of Anton," through the theatrical pathos of "Columbus and the Fat Lady," to the illusionist quasi realism of stories of rustic decay like "Brain Dust," "Country Music," and "Glass Eyes and Chickens," small masterpieces of the darker comedy in which the manifest eccentricity of the characters, which at times borders on insanity, is posed against a background of dismal verisimilitude. Deep in all these stories, whatever their manner and approach, is the sense of alienation that is strong in Cohen's novels as well, an alienation that goes far beyond Marx's socioeconomic use of the term to what the early nineteenth-century specialists in mental disorders meant when they called themselves alienists. In fictional terms this means a schizoid division, an inner split, in which a man is seen to be divided into two beings, and one cannot easily tell which is the real self and which the persona, which is Dr. Jekyll and which Mr. Hyde, and of the two, whether Hyde or Jekyll is dominant.

This problem appears as a division between role and personality in "The Cure." Eliot, the central character, is a rich psychotic obsessed with his relationship with his senile father but also, in a quasi-Marxian way, haunted by his own economic situation, so that he suddenly feels himself "to be no more than an attempt by his bank balance to project someone human, an account book to live in, the living shadow of his own money."[52] Eliot gets beyond his economic phobia by "curing" himself in a hysterical scene with his father when he tries to transfer to the old man the sense of madness he finds rising up within himself: "'I can't take you out,' he whispered, 'you're crazy.' And then he was shouting, 'You're crazy, YOU'RE FUCKING CRAZY'" (*NF*, p. 16). But what Eliot has in fact done is merely to confirm his alienation, to establish his exclusion from his own self.

The situation is "excellent," he tells his doctor, but: "The situation was in the centre of his mind, and from there he saw himself, absolutely inspired, so false he could have flown, raise one arm and place it, loose and familiar, on the shoulder of the doctor" (*NF*, p. 16).

In "Janice," one of the stories retained from *Columbus and the Fat Lady*, the phenomenon of inner division is treated in a more traditionally Gothic way. There is a trio consisting of Janice, the narrator Robert, and a mysterious Nicholas who is drowned, then survives to marry Janice, and finally fades into "Nicholas someone" (*NF*, p. 92), half-forgotten. Nicholas is clearly Robert's *Doppelgänger*, the feared other side of himself who must be destroyed; does he exist elsewhere than in the narrator's mind?

Yet another kind of division, between the physical self and the mental fantasy that usurps its functions, is developed in "Vogel." Storekeeper Sam Vogel tries to escape from death by following tuning-up programs and embarking on middle-aged sexual adventures. But in the end, it is only the form, not the fact, of his death that he changes. He dies, essentially, from the split between the inner self, represented by a twenty-five-year-old graduation photograph, and the new self, which he creates when the doctor tells him he must become athletic in order to survive. The new self "existed solely in his mind and was not something that could be seen. It was a sensation. The feel of his own body in flight, running: one foot on the ground, taking his whole weight and springing it back, while the other licked out front, confidently reaching" (*NF*, p. 45).

This new self "in the mind" is regressive and in fact turns into an old, forgotten self. Vogel lies like a child in his young mistress's bed, and he dies from a heart attack on the running track, "curled up like a baby on the special composition surface of the track" (*NF*, p. 45). Sam's death is a virtual journey into birth, just as his life had been a journey into death, a journey of forgetting the early self of the graduation photograph: ". . . whoever had lived inside that picture, whoever had walked around with whatever forgotten obsessions, had been buried in circumstance" (*NF*, p. 55).

Some of the stories in *Night Flights* are linked to Cohen's later and larger novels: "Columbus and the Fat Lady" to *The Colours of War*; and the country stories, like "Brain Dust," "Country Music," and "Glass Eyes and Chickens," to *The Disinherited* and *The Sweet Second Summer of Kitty Malone*. I shall discuss them later, but now I am concerned with the relationship between the three stories I have just delineated and Cohen's early novellas, *Korsoniloff* and *Johnny Crackle Sings*.

These are both tales of inner alienation, of that division of the self which can end only in permanent loss, and which exists always on the wavering verge of insanity. In *Korsoniloff*, the schizoid teacher of philosophy tells the history of his divided self — the separate lives of the cold and intrusive "I" and the ineffectually passionate and amoral half of himself he calls "Korsoniloff" — the ever-surgent elemental man. "Me cold? With my secret lusts and satanic nights. Me, my career turned upside down by Korsoniloff — who is nothing but a bundle of supercharged impulses? Cold?"[53] This is how the narrator speaks at one point in the novella. In another place, he declares, charting the currents of a divided being, "I lead my life; Korsoniloff leads his. From time to time there is a shift in the balance of forces; the 'I,' as it were, switches to the new prevailing direction" (p. 48).

"I" becomes detrimentally involved in the forces of society through the misdemeanours of Korsoniloff, who turns up at the marriage of their former mistress, Marie, disturbs the peace, and is brought before the courts. Korsoniloff sees the incident in the terms of his fantasy, "I" in the terms of uncomfortable reality. Marie had already, even before the wedding scene, shrewdly assessed her relationship with the "I" called Korsoniloff: "She looked at me and told me that before she had met me she had known no one deeply and had felt alone within herself but that now she felt not only alone but isolated and that she wasn't sure but that she preferred the first" (p. 62).

As the bathetic comedy of the trial goes on, we are not surprised to find "I" speculating: "Who was the master and who the pupil? I could see it both ways. For not only did I create Korsoniloff; Korsoniloff's existence transformed me" (p. 88). Behind this division of the self into alternately dominating personae, we reach, at the end, the unconscious guilt, submerged in amnesia, of the child who has seen his mother fall into the river, perhaps has even pushed her, and has immediately forgotten. "I," the ego, is the self-preserving censor of that past; Korsoniloff is the unconscious self in rebellious search of the truth that, once revealed, would destroy both him and "I."

The thematic sources of *Korsoniloff* in psychoanalytical theory are obvious. But the theories of neither Jung nor Freud ever created a good artist or ensured a polished miniature masterpiece like this first of Matt Cohen's books. The novella's intellectual translucency and strange, alabastrine unemotionality are artistic virtues, and, as I have already suggested, they relate Cohen more closely than any of his Canadian contemporaries to the ripples of the *nouvelle vague* that had originated in France a decade before.

Johnny Crackle Sings, Cohen's other early novella, is a more eccentric and personal book than *Korsoniloff*. It is as brilliant in its writing and as detached emotionally as *Korsoniloff*, yet in its madness it does not cling so closely to clinical verisimilitude. It was, as Cohen has remarked, the first of his books that he really "made . . . up" (Twigg, p. 177), and in its inventiveness it is as Canadian as its predecessor was European in feeling, and as temperamentally attached to the 1960s, which were ending as it was written so that it took on something of a threnodic tone, just as Cohen's later novels became merged in the long flow of history, or at least detached themselves from the novelist's own present.

The setting of *Johnny Crackle Sings* is the Ottawa Valley — rural eastern Ontario with its lingering Upper Canadian order breaking apart under the impact of urban influences. Johnny Harper, a high-school dropout, is built up by an unscrupulous and stupid local impresario into a pop singer with celebrity at the other end of his mental telescope. In fact he is doomed to failure, partly because of the self-destructive urge that makes him take so easily to drugs, but partly also because he lacks the talent that would make him struggle to survive. There is a strange, bittersweet flavour to the book as Cohen, tenderly but also sardonically, charts out Johnny's erratic and doomed career, upward to hallucinatory triumph, downward to actual failure, on to mental breakdown, to convalescence on a hippy farm in the Ottawa Valley, and back with a perverse insistence to the singing circuit that will destroy him.

The style of narration is oblique, and the narrative is deliberately discontinuous. Johnny's narcotically inspired fantasies alternate with the more factual narration of Lew Clinton, the civil servant turned farmer and medicine man who both encourages Johnny in drug-taking and saves him from the worst excesses, and with the newspaper reports of the Ottawa *Citizen* columnist, Frank Shaughnessy, who follows the highs and the more predictable lows of Johnny's singing career. As in *Korsoniloff*, and in so many of Cohen's short stories, one is constantly aware of the hero's inner division, in this case between Johnny the country boy, who a generation before might have been a happy farmer, and Johnny the disoriented product of the modern educational system, whose phony ambitions make him a victim of the kind of petty exploiters who preyed on and destroyed the creative impulses that stirred in the youth culture of the 1960s. *Johnny Crackle Sings* seemed a brilliant and timely experiment when it appeared in 1971, but its very closeness to the time and place have limited its appeal; its topicality faded, it was never reprinted, and today one reads it as a bright period piece, less relevant outside its own temporal setting than almost anything Cohen has written.

Cohen told Alan Twigg in an interview that during one period of about six months he was writing "the central parts" of *Johnny Crackle Sings*, of *Columbus and the Fat Lady*, and of *The Disinherited*. During this period, he added, "My writing totally changed. I had finally written through all the preconceptions I had about what writing was and just started writing about whatever it was that engaged me most deeply" (Twigg, p. 177).

Whatever may have happened in Cohen's mind and his consciousness, the divide that parts *The Disinherited*, as a final achievement, from the earlier works is quite evident. Though, as Cohen has told us, the basic idea of *The Disinherited* was conceived as early as 1970, the writing of *Johnny Crackle Sings* lay between its beginning and its completion, and so did the writing of the abandoned novel that showed Cohen the limits of his ability to return to traditional, linear forms.

Yet there are features of both *Korsoniloff* and *Johnny Crackle Sings* that linger on into the later, larger novels — particularly that uneasy feeling of existing unhappily between two worlds, ". . . one dead, / The other powerless to be born," which can only be resolved in fictional terms by accepting, and seeking to express, a sense of the constant interpenetration of past and present. The sense of ominous, and often disastrous, transition is present in all of Cohen's larger works: *The Disinherited*, *Wooden Hunters*, *The Colours of War*, *The Sweet Second Summer of Kitty Malone*, *Flowers of Darkness*, and even *The Spanish Doctor* with its very different setting. Orders that seem stable, like the agricultural economy of Upper Canada and the elaborately ceremonial culture of the British Columbia coastal Indians, collapse and leave their peoples disoriented, searching between a lost past and an unrealized future, until, in *The Colours of War*, the violence and despair already present in the earlier novels takes control, and, as society disintegrates, the direction of progress becomes a journey into the past. It is in this confusion that the characters reveal their divisions of purpose, the essential alienations that warp their natures. Yet, as *The Sweet Second Summer of Kitty Malone* suggests, and the final Kiev chapters of *The Spanish Doctor* do in a different way, the retreat from joy is not irreversible, even for those who have been most scarred by life.

Four of Cohen's larger novels — all except *Wooden Hunters* and *The Spanish Doctor* — are set in a southeastern Ontario countryside where Loyalists, later American immigrants, and the migrants who came from Britain after 1814 cleared the great forests where the *coureurs de bois* had once roamed, built themselves towns of stone and farmhouses fit to last for generations, and established a stable, prosperous farming economy that seemed eternal — and which lasted little more than a century before machine technology and urbanization turned it from a thriving way of life into an anachronistic flaw in the industrial pattern.

This countryside and its people are first introduced, in all their obsolescent decadence, in three short stories, all completed before *The Disinherited*, even if they were conceived at the same time. In each of these stories, the principal characters are two rustic drunkards, Pat and Mark Frank, who assume minor roles in *The Disinherited* and, in Pat's case, in *The Colours of War* and *Flowers of Darkness*, and major roles in *The Sweet Second Summer of Kitty Malone*, in which parts of the early stories appear in somewhat changed form. The Malone family, whose various members figure, or are mentioned, in all four novels, first appeared in the story "Brain Dust," and in this story we first enter Salem, the centre of Cohen's imaginary countryside. In *The Colours of War*, the old, stone, market town seems the epitome of rustic virtues and failings, and projects an eccentric sanity in a world of collective madness; in *Flowers of Darkness*, it is shown to be ridden by its own special, and equally destructive, frenzies.

The world of Salem is one where, as a character in "Country Music" remarks, "people . . . are terrible liars" (*NF*, p. 105), and where truth seems to shift according to the story and the teller, or perhaps in accordance with the author's view of its relativity. In "Country Music," which Cohen has identified as the seed story of the Salem epic, Pat and Mark are represented as being the sons of the widow Frank by a wandering, single-day lover named John MacRae. In "Glass Eyes and Chickens," and later in both *The Disinherited* and *The Sweet Second Summer of Kitty Malone*, we are told that they were reared by their widower father, Terry Frank. A prosperous farmer, Terry finally took to drink, and his farm, where Mark now lives by repairing decrepit trucks with bits of even more decrepit vehicles, serves as a paradigm of the land's decay and its submergence by the relentless advance of the machine, which in its turn is subject to decay:

> In the time of his [Mark Frank's] father's sobriety, there had been a white frame farmhouse surrounded by four barns, two hundred acres of only mildly rocky land, and a huge maple bush that backed down to the lake. Successive waves of alcoholism and fire had swallowed the land and burned down the original house. The new house was only the old pig barn in disguise; it was flanked by the two other remaining barns, which sat in front of it like twin warnings of disaster. Between them, leading from the house to the highway, was a hundred-yard driveway littered on either side with dead vehicles and spare parts, a true cornucopia of ancient and rusting cars and trucks. They filled the barnyard better than pigs or cows ever had. Like crops, they were planted from time to time and harvested when needed; but unlike crops, they demanded nothing, had no rhythm of their own, only the rhythm of his own days and whims. ("Glass Eyes and Chickens," in *NF*, p. 94)

This vision of transition and decay, shown in miniature in the stories, is projected, in *The Disinherited*, onto the wide screen of a novel in the classic manner, a rural, dynastic chronicle centred on the death of one member of the family and evoking the past of several generations through the apparently erratic, but really cumulative, operation of memory. The action is rich, largely because it is seen for the most part through the inner eye.

Early one morning, waking with a disturbing premonition, the farmer Richard Thomas, who is a neighbour and friend of the Frank brothers, goes out to inspect his property. He is felled by a stroke and taken to hospital, and there, when he is about to be released as at least partly cured, he dies of a second attack. As he lies in bed before his death, he remembers, and his memories, and the emotions rising from them, are complemented by those of his wife, his son, and his adopted son, and by their encounters during his time in hospital. There is a chronological succession on one level – from Richard's stroke to his death and burial, embracing the family conflicts over what will happen to the farm at his death. But the past emerges sporadically, in fragments, as associations create it or as it surges up out of the unconscious memory, and finally it clusters into a completeness that stands outside duration; a past that, because it is whole, is as depthless as a present. The process Cohen uses is similar to the process of recollective reconstruction that I remember taking place when I was recovering from a brief amnesia: some memories emerged with no apparent reason, and others were attracted to them by association, so that blocks of the past coalesced rather haphazardly, until, in the end, the whole jigsaw puzzle of lost time was filled in – all, that is, except the hours when I was in actual amnesia.

The pattern brought back from time by the end of the novel justifies its title, *The Disinherited*, though the disinheritance is mental rather than physical. It presents the history of the family founded by Richard Simon Thomas in the mid-nineteenth century, when he came to Ontario as the ancestral, earth-breaking pioneer. Vigorous and earthily amoral in their differing ways, Richard Simon Thomas and his son Simon and his grandson Richard carry on the farm in splendid style, each opening new fields in the rocky wilderness to satisfy his ambition. In their century of occupation, the holding assumes that illusive appearance of permanence, almost of antiquity, which the earlier-settled parts of Canada so quickly took on. But Canada has not, in fact, been allowed the slow growth from the mediaeval into the modern world, the long maturing that made the peasant order of Europe a matter of centuries, even of millennia. From beginning to end, our pioneer orders have been a matter of generations, even of decades.

By Richard's death in 1970, it is evident that the energy of the Thomas race, and its attachment to the land, are being sapped as surely as the land is being ruined by the creep of urbanization. Richard, who abandoned his university education to return to the farm, has held out obstinately against the offers of land speculators who wish to build summer cottages and a resort marina on the lakeshore of his property. But his son Erik, through whose mind the novel draws to a final close, is not interested in following his example. In a less extreme way, Erik resembles Korsoniloff, in that he is an apprentice academic with a divided will. The difference between the son and the father is shown in a key conversation in the hospital. Erik tries to justify his choice of a university career over an agrarian life that would keep the farm in the Thomas bloodline. Here, in about a page, is contained the thematic key to *The Disinherited*:

> "You know," Erik said, "that just because I don't want to live on the farm, it doesn't mean I didn't learn anything from you."
>
> "That's nice," Richard said.
>
> "It's just that, well, there's a lot of important things going on in this country and so, you know, people have to be able to think clearly. And the university is the place where that happens."
>
> "The rules . . ." Richard said, remembering a previous argument when Erik claimed that all logical thinking had rules.
>
> "Yes."
>
> "You teach people the rules," Richard said.
>
> "Yes."
>
> "What about life?"
>
> "What about it?"
>
> "Who teaches people how to live?"
>
> "I don't know," Erik said. Richard could tell he was starting to lose his temper. He had just put out one cigarette and was now lighting another, forgetting even to go and smoke it by the window. "People have to teach themselves how to live."
>
> "God help them," Richard said.
>
> "He never has," Erik up on his feet, pacing back and forth from window to door . . . . "People think well, all right, all they have to do is tend their own garden as best they can, never look beyond it, as if the world has stopped so they can do whatever they want, but it's not true, things have changed, the whole world is connected together."
>
> "It was always connected together," Richard said.
>
> "Politically."
>
> "That's what Hitler wanted."
>
> "God." Erik had sat down now, giving up entirely, looking as if he had decided he would sit there without speaking until either someone else came or Richard died, whichever came first, it didn't matter.
>
> "I'm sorry," Richard said. "I'm just an old man."

> "It doesn't matter."
> "But I've always thought there was more to life than rules or logic."
> "Of course," Erik said.
> "A man has to know his own destiny."
> "Oh Christ," Erik sighed, starting to get to his feet again and then slumping back into his chair. "No one has destinies anymore," he said. "They live in apartments and breed goldfish." It was early afternoon, just after lunch. The courtyard was emptier than ever, mid-August doldrums, and the sun shone flat and hot on the black asphalt. Around the edges of the courtyard, and slowly encroaching on the middle, were crumpled-up chocolate bar wrappers, old newspapers, crushed milkshake cartons. There were only a few cars parked there, all of them seeming dusty and familiar.[54]

No matter how he had tried to change him, Erik always "seemed city to Richard, the way he avoided things with his body, wore his clothes as decoration, was always glancing nervously around himself, as if there was something about to bite" (p. 187). Yet, even if he bears little resemblance to the earthy line of the Thomases, Erik does rather resemble, in his aloofness and his special sensitivity, the mystic poet, now become a legend, William C. Thomas, who came to live with Richard Simon Thomas, seduced his wife, and gave her as illegitimate son the mad and exalted Frederick Thomas; through reading the poet's journals, preserved by Frederick's half-brother Simon, Erik is finally able to sense a release from the family past against which William C. Thomas, like him, had in his own way rebelled, and to think of a new beginning.

The adopted son, Brian, disgusts Richard with his stupidity, yet he is "stronger and more capable" (p. 198) than Erik; he even bears a closer physical resemblance to Richard, and he turns out in the end to be the only possible heir. But even this situation produces its conflicts; Brian attacks Erik with a broken bottle at Richard's funeral, even though the farm has been left to him to run as long as he wishes. For the line between the sane and the alienated in *The Disinherited* is never so clearly drawn as one might expect. The rural existence is no guarantee of a balanced, or even a quiet, life. Richard and his father, Simon, fight almost to the death over Katherine Malone. And alienation is personified, not only in city-lost men like Erik, but also among the Franks and their companions, "drunk white witch doctors staggering around in the middle of winter passing through convulsions for this brief vision" (p. 155), who provide a chorus of sad buffoons for the life of Richard and his ancestors, just as the night nurse in the hospital, with her tales of grotesque sicknesses, provides the chorus to his death. The tragic and the bizarre are not remote from each other in Cohen's world.

In this chaotic pattern, the women play the role of reconciling the irreconcilables. Through lying in a barn with her husband's poet-cousin, Richard Simon Thomas' wife, Elizabeth, becomes the mother of the crazy Frederick Thomas, who is thus the half-brother of her legitimate son, the shrewd and vindictive Simon. Katherine Malone is the mistress of Simon and then Richard, the father and then the son. Richard's wife, Miranda, provides the only real bridge between him and their son Erik. And there is a strange link between Miranda and Erik through Rose Garnett, who seduces Erik when he encounters her living in a decayed farmhouse on a back-woods road, and who then surfaces as a well-connected fortune teller whom Miranda recommends to her son.

If Katherine Malone, so fertile that any encounter seems to make her pregnant, is the Demeter symbol of other-containment in *The Disinherited*, then Rose is the personification of self-containment, as perilous and enigmatic as the Jungian anima, unassailable, and aware of the bounds of other people's selfhood. When Erik suggested to her that they live together, ". . . she had ignored it, as if it was clear that he couldn't possibly mean such a thing, that he was obviously incapable of letting anything pass in or out of his own boundaries . . ." (p. 218).

When Erik does appear to achieve the kind of union with another person that takes him out of himself, it is with an unnamed, pregnant girl he meets and casually sleeps with, giving her the ring of the mystic poet, though he knows they will not live together. In all his actions, he projects the loneliness, the unrelenting alienation, of modern urban man, from which the very hazards of their way of life seem to shield the farming people who gathered at Richard Thomas' funeral and "mourned him without particular grief or feeling but as a necessary marking of their own passing" (p. 227).

The Disinherited is a work of vigour and density, in which the sense of warring past and present is splendidly created, and the characters of which leave massive shadows on the mind.

Cohen's second larger novel, *Wooden Hunters*, leaves Eastern Canada for a new terrain in the Queen Charlotte Islands off British Columbia's Pacific coast. The island of the novel, which is unnamed, is inhabited by the survivors of the great Haida nation, who live side by side with itinerant loggers and lifestyle refugees from the straight world. It is a place where nature appears irrepressible, constantly self-renewing:

> The alder silhouetted against the blue sky, the coloured leaves and frozen morning reminded him of the east but the wetness and fertility of this island, the newness of the air, the speed with which things seemed to grow and then be re-absorbed into the forest floor all made the east seem used and impossible to him, a place that could no longer renew itself, and now sometimes he imagined that whole section of the continent as a vast conglomerate city of doomed smokestacks and concrete.[55]

This sense of decay and everlasting renewal reconcile the characters with the setting, for all the people we meet in *Wooden Hunters* have lost or forsaken their pasts, and, unlike the characters in *The Disinherited*, they know it.

The Indians have left their native villages and abandoned their magnificent culture; the mouldering totem poles symbolize their predicament, and it is personified in Johnny Tulip, drunken, drug-drenched, and sustaining his last months of life playing old jazz tunes on the warped piano in the local hotel:

> Johnny Tulip laughed his crazy broken laugh, laughed and then coughed again. It seemed impossible to Calvin that this man could have a past, or at least a past other than what he carried with him, marked into his body and face, so much his own now that other people's mistakes could no longer touch him. (p. 20)

Yet the past is there, permeating both present and future. By their converging pasts, such incongruous people as the wandering intellectual, Calvin ("a weak but persistent moth" [p. 20], as he sees himself), the renegade middle-class Vancouver girl, Laurel Hobson (Calvin's lover and once Johnny Tulip's), and the hotel manager, C. W. Smith from Montana, with his undertaker's clothes and the hearse he drives around the island, are brought together on this ultimate edge of North America, this last of frontiers, this margin beyond civilization where nature is still strong enough to threaten, and where the old wars between traditions are yet unstilled. Smith thinks he has "slipped away from his past, eluded it in some secret and final way" (p. 79), but it is lying in wait to reclaim him, and eventually does, just as, despite Johnny's air of self-containment, he has never ceased to be an Indian.

Wooden Hunters is constructed to take account of the reality of the past, since, like *The Disinherited*, it follows a general forward movement in time, punctuated by flashes of memory, though the time recovered in this way is not so rich as in the earlier novel, for *Wooden Hunters* does not set out to create a dynastic record; its aim is to release the tensions of a violent present.

The memory patterns which Cohen uses in *Wooden Hunters* to project the personalities and the personal histories of the characters differ considerably in scope and intensity. Calvin, in fact, has few memories; his accounts of his parents and his childhood are meagre, and his recollections really come alive only after he encounters Laurel Hobson, having left his life in the East to discover a new existence, perhaps a new personality, in the West. This limitation in memory accords with his sense of starting afresh, almost as ineffectual as a child, in this new and harsh environment, where he feels he can survive only by a self-transformation he has not yet attained. He is too much involved in this process of becoming to be greatly concerned with what happened to him in the past.

Laurel Hobson, who is his mentor as well as his lover, and who, in her self-containment, resembles Rose in *The Disinherited*, has transformed herself and survived. The process began with her first visit to the island six years earlier as an innocent, to be seduced by Johnny, and then to break her spine falling down a cliff. She can afford to remember because she now accepts the apparent accidents that have changed her life. As she recovers in Vancouver from her almost fatal injuries, she finds the middle-class life she had known so insipid that she returns to the island, takes over an abandoned cabin, and learns to become a ruthless hunter. She indeed sets the pattern of violence in the opening pages of the novel by initiating Calvin into the brutal West Coast practice of pitlamping — shooting a deer at night by holding it in the fascination of a flashlight beam. Laurel is wild and degenerate at the same time, scarred by long sessions of alcohol and morphine and cocaine, yet also tough and resilient, mentally and bodily. The breaking and knitting of her spine seems to symbolize the remaking of her personality, just as, in *The Disinherited*, the breaking of Rose Garnett's spine preceded an inner transformation. When Calvin looks at Laurel, he thinks:

> Despite everything that was animal about her she always seemed entirely rational to him, each action thought out and consecutive, one day following the other in some great inevitable framework whose shape was known to her, if no one else, its existence guaranteed by the absolute conviction with which she did everything . . . . (p. 32)

If one accepts the thesis of Margaret Atwood's *Survival*, there is something typically Canadian in Laurel's learning to live with sang-froid in her cruel and tender world. But Cohen's study of Camus alerts one to a pattern often encountered in the novels of European absurdists: the deliberate courting of extreme situations in which, by choices made in the face of death (one's own or other men's or that of creatures like deer and salmon brutally slaughtered), one recreates oneself. For there is a clearly triumphal quality to Laurel, despite her scarred body and mind, that counterpoints the elegiac music of Johnny Tulip's inevitable decline, trapped in the collective tragedy of his people. It is with Calvin that Laurel chooses to stay, after Johnny's mother has promised them a "good future" seen through the "luminous wooden eyeball[s]" (p. 219) of her blindness — Calvin who has come west, making his mind a tabula rasa on which he could lose but also find himself: "In the spring they would explore the coast, live on mussels and clams, make salads of wild peas and plantain" (p. 218).

There is the suggestion at the end of *Wooden Hunters* that by immersion in the eternal present of natural ways of living, the cycle of violence can be brought to an end. But in *The Colours of War*, Theodore Beam, who has drifted to the West Coast, like Calvin, in search of a freer and perhaps more natural life, discovers, under the hard fists of police thugs at the beginning of the novel, that even this outpost is not exempt from the social war sweeping over North America late in our century. As a figure for the conflict of generations and ways of life, war plays its part in *The Disinherited*. It moves sharply towards literal reality in *Wooden Hunters*, when Johnny greets Laurel with the mysterious remark "It's war" (p. 64) and leads her into the woods to destroy the giant tractor which C. W. Smith and the logging company have taken into the forest to start a massive timber operation that will destroy the site of an old Indian village beside a deserted inland lake. This act initiates a miniature war when Smith retaliates by blowing up the mortuary poles in the village and then is killed, as the Indians are about to riot in his hotel, by a psychotic youth who has driven his hearse over from the mainland. That round of warfare, directed against the exploitative materialism of Smith and the logging company, dies down as the survivors go on with their personal lives and deaths. But the conflict of *The Colours of War* is no longer episodic; it has become a general condition of the times.

The action of *The Colours of War* takes place in a future that is not very distant, since characters out of *The Disinherited*, like Katherine Malone and Pat Frank, have survived to take part in it. The action is built around a bizarre journey that extends spatially across Canada from Vancouver to Salem, Ontario, but which is also a journey through time. To the reader, Theodore seems to be travelling in the future; but, in fact, he is on his way back into the past. Once again, *The Colours of War* is a memory novel, and as Theodore journeys, past, present, and future mingle like the colours of a shaken kaleidoscope.

Living the easy life without destination that still seems possible on the Pacific Coast, Theodore — whose father is a Jewish newspaper editor in Salem — becomes dimly aware that social life is breaking down all over North America. Hunger has at last begun to afflict even the affluent lands, disorder follows hunger, and governments react in the only way that governments can: "Every day it seemed there were new declarations of emergencies and martial law. Not exactly a new war: things being the same as always but carried one step further."[56] One day the irrational hand of power reaches out to Theodore. Two detectives invade his flat, rough him up, and ransack his rooms, but he is not sure whether they have come in search of the cocaine, which his Chinese landlady deftly removes from their sight, or for something mysterious that he does not in fact possess. It is his birthday, and that night his father rings from Salem. Theodore accepts Jacob Beam's urgings to return home, but the journey that takes him back to his past, and, in a sense, to Canada's past, goes by way of a future that threatens us all. He reaches the station and finds it packed with people responding to obscure fears and self-preservatory urges:

> Not only were the departing trains completely booked, but the station was further swollen with those who were arriving. And for every one of us who was fleeing to some more certain home in the East, it seemed there were several who hoped that the mild wet winters of the Coast would be easier to survive. I was reminded again of old stories of the depression and the vast armies of the unemployed criss-crossing the country; when nothing else is possible, motion promises to fill the stomach. (p. 36)

The train on which Theodore manages to book a compartment turns out to be no ordinary train. Among the coaches packed with bona fide travellers, there are also sealed vans, filled with arms and ammunition and controlled by a group of guerrillas. By chance, Theodore has already encountered the partisan leader, Christopher Perestrello, in the station restaurant. "His [Perestrello's] voice and features were so strong he seemed almost dangerous, even cruel: not the careless cruelty of the police but something more purposeful" (p. 38).

Like Katherine Malone and Pat Frank, Perestrello brings in an echo from earlier Cohen writings, and especially from "Columbus and the Fat Lady." This is the story of a fairground performer who trades on his psychoses by living out on stage a tranced fantasy of having been Columbus, and who dies in the middle of his performance — or appears to do so. His wife, like the wife of the original Columbus, is named Felipa Perestrello, and the wife of Perestrello (who bears the name of Christopher) in *The Colours of War* is also Felipa, while the town of Salem, we later learn, was founded by a descendant of the Francisco de Bobadilla who, in 1500, arrested Columbus and his son Diego. Christopher Perestrello, as it turns out, is obsessed with the consequences of Columbus' discovery of America and is dedicated to reversing them. He is a Columbus enlightened and repentant.

When Theodore first sees him, Perestrello is attacked by a stranger, and the police escort the two of them out of the station restaurant. Theodore picks up an envelope Perestrello has left on the table. It contains a map of the route the train is following, marked at certain points with sites of rendezvous. Theodore's possession of the map leads him into contact with the partisans, for in the bar car on the train he meets a girl named Lise who takes him to her room and later threatens him with a pistol and demands the map.

Theodore becomes Lise's lover, learns of her long connection with groups seeking to undermine North American governments, and realizes the true function of the train, which Perestrello has organized through his railway union contacts to distribute arms to partisan groups all over the country and spread rebellion in its wake. Theodore joins the partisan group and is present when the citizen soldiers of Regina, mobilized by the government to preserve order, go over to Perestrello. The one farmer who opposes is shot outside the hotel as Theodore watches:

> And standing at this window, looking out at this scene, we might have been anywhere, in any of dozens of cities that have seen revolutions and coups, reprisals and executions.
>
> . . . .
>
> I had always thought that the external world would plod along forever, unchanged — a comfortable and amorphous bureaucracy, surrounding my life like a giant marshmallow, a giant excuse. Now that was fading away and I was beginning to feel responsible for every moment I lived. (pp. 131, 132)

As the train goes on, stopping several times every night for crates of weapons to be unloaded, Theodore feels as if it were "turning itself into a long metal arrow drawing together the endless years of strikes, shortages, summer riots, outbursts of violence, into one spectacular collision" (p. 148). He is never sure whether the partisans are involved in a general uprising in which unions and army may combine to take over the country, or whether Perestrello is merely travelling like Columbus into a great unknown, hoping his journey will coincide with outside events to make a revolutionary situation.

All through the journey, in dreams and reveries, Theodore is returning to the past that Salem — daily drawing nearer — represents for him. His most evocative memory concerns a childhood visit to his Orthodox Jewish grandfather. He looks at the strange, gnome-like, ancient man and sees "the pale blue eyes that I recognized as my eyes but a thousand years old, my eyes shining out of his face" (pp. 153–54).

> As I lay in bed and waited for sleep, I held a secret in my mind — that my grandfather and I were the same person, that I had seen myself in the mirror of the glass door, then the door had opened and he stepped out: me in disguise. (p. 154)

Here is the theme of the haunting *Doppelgänger* representing the division of self that appears in Cohen stories like "Janice," but also the concern for tradition and continuity already developed in *The Disinherited*; the grandfather's gift to Theodore is time, objectified in a gold watch, thin and old.

Even Perestrello is really entering the future to find the past, as all the great revolutionaries have tried to do. In the last scene in which he is actually present, he talks of "pure force" (p. 157), not merely as the urge of modern revolutionaries, but also as the urge that brought people from the Old to the New World. Having destroyed Europe, men came to the Americas, where, this repentant Columbus tells us, ". . . before we came, men lived as true men, and every human knew the meaning of his own life" (p. 157). The land was waiting, to be "take[n] for our own" (p. 158).

> Perestrello shrugged and leaned further over the table and the map this world had become. "Of course, we were wrong. The future was only the past in an elaborate disguise. The continent was ruined as easily as a child or a wife. With the slaves and the killings we poisoned ourselves. We began to realize that the new world had already become the old. There was no place to receive us. We could only go round and round, repeating ourselves.
>
> "I still have hope," Perestrello said. "Somewhere inside us there's a place that has never been touched, and is still innocent, waiting to be discovered. When we've suffered, when the violence is over and the false governments have fallen, when we're simple men and women again, standing on the face of the earth, there'll be something we can reach for, something noble inside us." (pp. 158–59)

Perestrello is a creature of the time of violence, and does not survive into an age of innocence regained. It soon becomes evident that all is not so completely under his control as it appeared. Felipa is attacked on the train by double agents; Perestrello himself is wounded by a sniper when the train stops to deliver arms; news comes that government troops have suppressed the insurgents in Regina and Vancouver; and finally, the train reaches a railway yard in Ontario where army units await it with artillery. Perestrello is killed in the battle. Theodore and Lise escape, and so, independently, does Felipa.

Theodore and Lise make their way to Salem. The town is filled with government troops, whom Theodore fears, yet there are hilarious bibulous interludes with Jacob Beam, Pat Frank, and other town characters before Theodore takes refuge in an abandoned country church belonging to Katherine Malone, now an octogenarian. Katherine survives as the personification of a simpler, surer world, which her old house and the old church even more solidly represent. And in the church, Theodore lives on, after Felipa has appeared and led Lise away to become an urban guerrilla. Hiding from the soldiers, he writes the book we are reading, until, in the last pages of the novel, Lise returns:

> Once we dreamed of being citizens in a perfect state. The cells of our body ran wild with faith, pushing us through childhood to this place we have reached. I remember the dreams; but sometimes it can't be helped — I hear not music but armies moving in the night.
>
> The earth will try to feed us, no matter how foolish we are. Soon Jacob Beam will sit out in the garden in the afternoons, feeling his eyes go blind, the sun crossing his face.
>
> Old words flood through me. This hand records them — my hand, my father's hand.
>
> The sky is clear and the sun is out. I can see Lise walking across the field, a rifle in her arms. For this day there is food again.
>
> We will go on living here. (pp. 233–34)

Through inaction, Theodore has regained the innocence Perestrello sought in vain through action.

Some aspects of *The Colours of War* render it ineffectual as a novel conceived in traditional terms. Perestrello is a figure whose mind we never really enter. Encased in his impeccable uniform, he is remote even from the other characters. Lise and Felipa are types of naïve and cynical radicalism, the sacred and profane poles of political enthusiasm. All three might be members of a dream, of which the train is the vehicle, and Matt Cohen has, in fact, been accused of populating his book with mannequins.

By the same criterion, the King of Brobdingnag in *Gulliver's Travels*, and even O'Brien in *Nineteen Eighty-Four*, might also be dismissed as mannequins because they are not developed and credible as human beings. But their functions are quite different from those of novelistic characters, and so are those of Perestrello and the two women in *The Colours of War.* Theodore can be seen as a kind of latter-day Candide, set to wander as an innocent through the man-made jungles of the present, and to find that all the promises of the future are illusory in comparison with the rediscovery of roots and of Cohen's wry equivalent of Voltaire's cultivation of one's garden. It is, like Voltaire's, a counsel of defiance rather than defeat, a statement of life continuing tenaciously in the ruin of social order and of political idealism. *The Colours of War* is, in its conclusions, luminous and salutary.

While *The Disinherited* shows modernization dislocating the agrarian culture of Canada and dispossessing its inhabitants spiritually as well as physically, and *The Colours of War* shows a future when progress has gone into retreat and men seek refuge in defensive nostalgia, *The Sweet Second Summer of Kitty Malone* reaches, through its creation of an intensely living present, a brilliantly and credibly positive conclusion. It translates the myths of popular fiction by showing that splendid romantic passions can belong to the lifeworn and ugly as well as to the young and beautiful, and that love can survive anger, defeat, and degeneration and can somehow squeeze from them joy.

The Sweet Second Summer must have been long in Cohen's mind, for two of the stories which, in 1978, he included in *Night Flights* find their way with very little alteration into the novel. These are "Brain Dust" and "Glass Eyes and Chickens," and the latter had already appeared in *Harrowsmith* in 1976. These stories not only evoke Salem's declining farming hinterland, but also include three of the novel's leading figures, Kitty Malone herself and the ageing twins Pat and Mark Frank, the "drunk white witch doctors" of *The Disinherited*. Kitty is the cousin of Joe Malone, whose wife, Katherine, was the lover of both Simon and Richard Thomas in that earlier novel, and her brother Charlie is the Frank brothers' closest friend.

In *The Sweet Second Summer*, Pat Frank is already an adult and a seasoned drunkard when Kitty, still a teenager, seduces him in the dreaming hayfields north of Kingston. In spite of her manifest infatuation, he refuses to marry her because he thinks it will be her destruction; secretly he believes that his brain is shrinking and that the voids left in his skull are filling up with dust. Kitty goes off to Toronto and marries a city slicker, Randy Blair. But she never entirely sheds her infatuation for Pat Frank, and inevitably the marriage fails. She returns to Salem to live in the house her grandfather built for his retirement before he fell to his death from the barn roof, and takes up again with Pat for another twenty years of haphazard shacking-up, from which she has a daughter, Lynn. Kitty's father has been killed in a car accident, her mother has retreated into merry senility, and Kitty has become a lonely woman as she has moved from a girlhood during which she was curious about life and death and destiny to an uncertain adulthood:

> She could remember being a girl, sidling about the kitchen floor in search of a warm spot, looking at her mother in the chair and wondering why she was sitting, not standing; why one day did it rain and others sun; why had her father died and been wrenched out of her life.
>
> She had spent whole days outside inspecting things for the certainty of their existence: examining trees to see why their leaves grew out of one place, not another; staring at the hay stacked in the barn and trying to figure out why it had been piled up one way, not another; going to look at the cows and trying to guess which would be the first to give up its grazing and sink onto its belly in the warm grass.
>
> Over the years she had watched the empty places left by her father's death fill up with herself, with her own uncertainty; and it seemed this uncertainty had always been there, just waiting to be tapped. It travelled from her heart and her mind to her body. As she changed from a girl into a woman her blond hair grew dry and crinkly, angling away from her head, and even her eyes became anxious and uncertain, never holding to anything or anyone for more than a few seconds before shifting away, making the rounds to check that nothing else essential was about to change.[57]

It is only when she has finally surrendered the possibilities and illusions of youth that Kitty can really find herself. She goes into hospital to have a cyst removed in an operation that renders her sterile; at the same time, Pat, at forty-nine already a skeletal alcoholic, fights the last battle of his belligerent career and is beaten up by Randy — her city-born son — and his father. It is now that Pat and she come together — lived-out wrecks by most standards, yet filled with an inexplicable access of youthfulness that sets Pat dreaming he is a boy again — to marry and share the same decaying farmhouse, and Kitty can find herself, in the last words of the novel, "standing straight, ready to live out the warm endless summer ahead" (p. 233).

What gives *The Sweet Second Summer of Kitty Malone* its special sense of depth and authenticity, despite a plot that might easily have turned sentimental, is Cohen's power of encompassing individual fates, and inescapable relationships like that of Kitty and Pat, within collective and ancestral patterns. In *The Disinherited*, there is the lineage of the Thomases, from the original great-grandfather down to Richard's town-corrupted son, Erik, to provide the background of a changing Canada within which the characters create and suffer and die, and the same applies to *The Colours of War*, where Theodore Beam's scarcely credible adventures are given substance, not by the utopian dreams of his doomed fellow conspirators, but rather by the long family vistas into the past provided by his father, Jacob, who had fought in Spain, and by his aged, Orthodox Jewish grandfather.

The age of a land is validated only by the human lineages with which it is identified, and so, in *The Sweet Second Summer*, it is the Malone ancestry — attached to the Malone lands — that forms the essential background to the strange romance of middle-aged Kitty and decrepit Pat, the ambiance within which these unlikely figures come to "calm of mind all passion spent." The lineage extends from the grandfather who fell to death from the barn, through Kitty's crazy mother, Ellen, who dies in an ecstatic vision of earthly love and union with God as she is visiting Kitty in hospital (while, in a kind of holy irony, a drunken Pat shouts, "Hallelujah!" [p. 169]), and down to Kitty's daughter by Pat — enigmatic Lynn, who dreams always of places beyond the places where men live.

Against the quixotic world of Perestrello and his fellow conspirators in *The Colours of War*, Cohen presents, in *The Sweet Second Summer of Kitty Malone*, a kind of Sancho Panza world, where survival is the great virtue. In that world, men appear to be selfish, taken up with minor greeds, irrational prides, and divisive longings, but the call of human need spreads out in great ripples from single passionate relationships to the strength of families and communities. In *The Sweet Second Summer of Kitty Malone*, it is most dramatically illustrated in the funeral of old Ellen, who had so impressed the people of Salem with her eccentric presence that the cemetery is densely packed, and people come in hundreds to drink away her life insurance at the wake, which is also the wedding party for Kitty and Pat. Here, at least, it is appropriate that the funeral baked meats should furnish forth the marriage table. For the strange ecstasy of Ellen's dying is not far removed from the strange ecstasy of Kitty's loving a man so doomed as Pat. Paradoxically, death at this point holds our minds in a celebration of life, of which the most striking image is Pat's epiphany as he walks home drunk from the wedding-wake:

> Tonight, though every inch of the path was known to his shoes, and knew them, Pat's perception was different. In the now-rising light he saw the bursts of spring leaves and the twisted remains of the maple forest anew, as if with each second of dawn it was growing again, painted into the clear morning air with no past at all, no previous image; painted into the clear morning air so new and clean he could suddenly smell the deep valley of oxygen rushing between the trunks. He turned and looked behind him: to the east the sky was showing a faint wash of pink, and the upper reaches of leaves were turning a bright and tender green with the first touch of sun.
>
> He was trembling. He could feel his heart beating faster, dizzy, stuttering and trying to open up, but this time it was not pouring out love. It was not burning with love, or need, or hate, or regret: just open, dizzily neutral. On the brink of falling over he stood and trembled, not daring even to move his hands towards his cigarettes; froze and gradually felt the day begin to suck into him: at first wispy and faint, then in a rushing torrent that pounded in his chest and rose up in his spine until it washed right through his skull, the sun lighting up and beaming through his eyes. For a moment he saw it blinding white and bursting with pure waves of life, life translucent waiting to be formed. And then he blinked and it was

> gone, the forest returned dark and enclosing, the few glowing patches of sky still dotted with stars. (pp. 216–17)

There is a kind of Dionysiac idyllicism about *The Sweet Second Summer*, but Dionysus was a chthonian god, a god from underground, and it is the more malign aspects of the world of instinct he rules over that tend to dominate Cohen's fifth novel, *Flowers of Darkness*, whose very title suggests the subterranean gardens of Persephone, the queen of Hades. So far as the writer — and the reader — is concerned, there is a Baudelairean feeling of moving into realms beyond good and evil, and perhaps it is not entirely an accident that the novel's title resembles so closely that of Baudelaire's central work, *Les Fleurs du mal*.

Flowers of Darkness is the Salem novel in which the town moves into full centre. In *The Colours of War* it was a destination, even though the last third of the book took place there. In *The Sweet Second Summer of Kitty Malone* and the country stories, it was peripheral to the rustic life of the characters. But in *Flowers of Darkness* it becomes the focus of the novel, complete with its own dominant symbols of the good and the evil, of righteousness and sin:

> Allen's office was in an old stone building on one of Salem's two downtown streets. At the southern end of these two streets, rising over and surveying the town and its inhabitants, was the Church of the New Age. In earlier eras it had been called Presbyterian, and then Methodist, but the name changes were only incidental, like new coats of paint. What stayed constant was the church's meaning, because it was placed at the edge of the stores as if to say: corruption — this far and no farther.
>
> At the other end of the town, facing the farm and bushland to the north, was the town's other main institution. This building had neither spire nor stone, but was a low, sprawling log structure, since covered by clapboard. It was the town's hotel and tavern. Its name also changed, sometimes by the generation and sometimes by the year, but its meaning too was constant: a fortress of comfort that stood between civilization and the terrifying wilderness.
>
> Between the poles of tavern and church Salem's inhabitants swayed or sometimes staggered.

> "You know," Finch had told Annabelle as he was leaving Donna's house, "there is a saying that in this town a man's life is taken up with the trip from one end to the other. If you get my meaning."
>
> "I get it, Mr. Finch."
>
> "And I'll tell you another thing, Mrs. Jamieson, if you don't mind me speaking in symbols, but God chooses very few to swim against the current."[58]

God's choices, inscrutable as always, make Salem the stage on which is acted out a drama of sin and retribution, with destiny arranged as inexorably as it ever was in the plays of Aeschylus and Sophocles. For if the characters in *The Sweet Second Summer of Kitty Malone* finally make their own true choices and in a classic existentialist way shape their destinies, in *Flowers of Darkness* they allow destiny to make the choices and turn possibility into fate.

There is a way in which, though it is set in an earlier and apparently more stable decade, *Flowers of Darkness* continues from *The Colours of War. The Colours of War* ends with Theodore Beam hiding out in the old stone church on the edge of town. *Flowers of Darkness* begins with the grocer, George Mandowski, peeping through the window of the same church and witnessing the seduction of seventeen-year-old Nellie Tillson by Gordon Finch, the pastor of the Church of the New Age. From this incident, the dark comedy and the eventual Gothic tragedy of the novel take their courses.

Cohen's series of Salem novels is united by setting and, to a great extent, by feeling, but, unlike a multivolume work like John Galsworthy's *The Forsyte Saga*, it does not maintain a constant cast of characters undergoing changing experiences. Major characters from one novel may be allowed to play minor roles in another, as Jacob Beam from *The Colours of War* and Pat Frank from *The Sweet Second Summer* do in *Flowers of Darkness*, but the main cast of this last novel is new: the philandering Reverend Finch and his beautiful wife, Maureen, who is crippled by arthritis; George Mandowski; and the Jamiesons, Annabelle and Allen, a lawyer and his ceramicist wife who have gone to earth in Salem until the memory of his legal improprieties can fade in the minds of his former fellow citizens in Ottawa. Unlike Pat Frank and Kitty Malone, these are people who seem favoured in life; nobody is crazed by drink, nobody is poor, the three leading women — Annabelle, Maureen, and Nellie Tillson — are all beautiful; both Jamieson and Finch are in a sense delinquent, yet they hold positions that make them envied by the world.

The images of Salem are dual and reflect the division in the hearts of the people. The Jamiesons have come there because the neat, old, stone houses give a sense of order, of a place where one can "leave the scandal behind," where ". . . he could be trusted and grow close to the people in the community while she took advantage of the slower rhythm of life to spend more time on her pottery" (p. 55). But, in fact, Salem is far from being this place of quiet retreat; Cohen's use, as an epigraph, of Wilde's saying "Anyone can be good in the country" is strictly ironic. Below its sleepy surface, Salem seethes with hatred and intrigue; its appearance of being divided between God's realm, represented by Finch's church, and Satan's realm, represented by the hotel at the other end of the town, is in fact quite deceptive, for the compelling powers of human desire — the roots, if not the flowers, of darkness — move equally in both realms.

The same contrast between the conscious yearning after order and the half-conscious acceptance of a necessary disorder exists in the characters, and particularly in the passionate Annabelle and the lustful Finch. Annabelle is no ordinary potter, content with plates and pitchers; she sees herself as somewhat like God, who "made Adam out of clay" (p. 54), when she sets about filling with figures representing Salem people a vast mosaic, which she explains will depict "the human condition, the agony and the ecstasy, the glorious, suffering, wonderful ordeal and history of mankind" (p. 55). And Finch too, as his wife, Maureen, sees, "had won his monkhood": ". . . in his own twisted way he had taken the world around him and squeezed it until it fitted the shape of his soul" (pp. 186–87). There is an appropriateness in the coming together of these characters who seek to imitate God; they share, among other things, their hubris.

And, like a punishment, in each case domination becomes enslavement. Finch, the hypocritical whoremaster, sees his amorous life as something he is condemned to, a sentence of servitude. Annabelle, for all her urban and urbane self-assurance, is caught in the same servitude when she becomes the lover of this stable-smelling hot gospeller. Yet the real pattern of destiny is carried on in the action of characters outside this central passionate relationship, which, in the dark irony of the book's ending, is revealed as almost an irrelevance, the accidental intrusion of a "city woman," as Finch mockingly calls

Annabelle, into the turbid currents of rural existence.

It is, in fact, submissive Nellie Tillson, made pregnant in the old church, who becomes the still centre of the drama. Mandowski and Finch's other enemies seek to destroy Finch by persuading Nellie to bring a paternity suit. Finch thinks he has turned the tables when he preaches a passionate *mea culpa*, begging the town's indulgence for his transgression, and the congregation hysterically shouts forgiveness. But Maureen, the white-skinned, red-haired beauty who once loved horses, has a pride which cannot endure such public humiliation. She borrows a revolver from Mandowski — who is infatuated with her — and kills Finch, then Mandowski, then herself. Annabelle, the survivor, the "city woman" whose affair with Finch has affected the main tragedy neither way, is left to discover that the only refuges are "absolutely private and removed" (p. 251), reaching into the individual consciousness.

More than any other of Cohen's novels, it is *Flowers of Darkness* that reminds one of the American novel of the South. There is a kind of theatricality with exaggerated lights and shadows, such as one encounters often in Faulkner; characters such as Maureen with her indoor white beauty, her flaming hair, and her passion for horses, and Finch, with his cavalier rendering of the preacher's role, have a combination of splendour and squalor one encounters often in Yoknapatawpha County. Yet it is high parody rather than imitation that we are witnessing. Cohen is using the Faulknerian elements as counters in his own melodramatic game.

Two things strike one most about *Flowers of Darkness*, and they are interconnected. First, there is the luminous clarity of description. One sees Salem and its people with the vivid and detailed sharpness of Pre-Raphaelite art. But, secondly, just as in Pre-Raphaelite painting one senses that the people represented are entranced in some strange vision world, so in *Flowers of Darkness* the characters seem to move, like the figures in an Aeschylus tragedy, along some dark road of the inevitable. They are not really free beings. They are shaped to their fates like Annabelle's clay puppets. And they destroy themselves because they remain the same. As characters they do not grow; at most they are progressively revealed to us as the novel proceeds. And so they are larger than life yet in some pathetic way less than human. In contrast, the characters of *The Sweet Second Summer* are human to the heart, and one can perhaps see the two novels as representing Cohen's vision of what can be nearest to heaven on earth and what is nearest to hell.

Cohen's most recent book as I end this essay is likely to strike readers — as it did critics at the time of publication — as a surprising and uncharacteristic work. *The Spanish Doctor* (1984) is set in the fifteenth century, when the Middle Ages were melting into the Renaissance, and it exchanges Salem, Ontario, for a sweep of European cities that begins with Toledo and proceeds through Montpellier and Bologna to Kiev.

This shift from the contemporary chronicles of rural backwaters that Cohen made his speciality in the Salem novels to a historical novel on the most lavish scale would probably take a great deal of critical ingenuity to explain if the author himself had not given us some clues in an essay he wrote for the twenty-fifth anniversary issue of *Canadian Literature*, entitled "Notes on Realism in Modern English-Canadian Fiction," and if he had not published in 1983 what one must regard as a transitional collection of stories, *Café Le Dog*. (He had published in 1982 a retrospective collection of earlier short fiction entitled *The Expatriate: Collected Short Stories*, which included all the stories already assembled in *Columbus and the Fat Lady* and *Night Flights*, in addition to the hitherto unpublished and banally enigmatic title story.)

In "Notes on Realism," Cohen talks of the dearth of experimental novelists in Canada, which he attributes to the fact that "the Canadian reality is a discontinuous one in terms of history." Unlike the Old World, where "the history of human alteration of the landscape" runs parallel to "the history of the various peoples and empires that lived there," change in Canada was "rapid and drastic." It was not made by "those who had habitually lived there," but "by settlers from across the ocean," bringing ideas "that had originated elsewhere."[59]

What Cohen has done in his new novel — a bold experiment that makes good use of traditional means — is to leap outside the limits of Canadian fiction as we generally understand it and write a novel that is not merely European in setting and period but also in theme and attitude. For *The Spanish Doctor* is the story of a man — Avram Halevi — drawn unwillingly into a spiritual quest that epitomizes the destiny of his people, the Jews, and the fate of those who resist uniformity. The drive to uniformity is exemplified by Cardinal Rodrigo Velásquez, the Roman church's most formidable and malign representative.

It is at this point that we should pause to consider *Café Le Dog*'s transitional function, and the way it shows the manifest veering of Cohen's interests and his growing acceptance of the need — foreshadowed in *The Colours of War* — to give voice to his Jewish inheritance. The collection consists of a novella, "Golden Whore of the Heartland," which takes up a third of the book, and seven stories. Though some are set entirely or partly in the country, Salem does not figure in this volume, and in the only wholly rural story, "A Love for the Infinite," the contact between the protagonist and the environment is wholly destructive.

Several of the stories — "Life on This Planet," "At the Empress Hotel," and "Café Le Dog" — are about failed artists, or perhaps rather nonartists, who live within pretentious artistic personae, and these — I believe — reflect a preoccupation with reaching the ultimate edge of literary authenticity, a preoccupation that may have led Cohen to abandon the imaginary country of Salem and its decaying farms, which he presented with an outsider's irony, and to take up as his next fictional territory the history of his own people, with its wealth of event and its depth of passion.

In this connection, one observes that most of the stories in *Café Le Dog* are concerned with people moving on, either from place to place or from relationship to relationship, and that often the shift is from Canada to some more cosmopolitan setting or partnership. The crucial scene in the title story, which concerns a failed Canadian poet living an aimless life in Paris as the friend of a spoiled courtesan, is the sudden arrival of the poet's mother at the Café Le Dog. Aged and just released from a mental home in Canada, she had set off on a journey whose ending she does not foresee, and her rejection of the past that has been haunting her son liberates him as well to find the meaning of life in the foreign city where he had dwelt a decade as a stranger.

The novella, "Golden Whore of the Heartland," concerns shifting personal relations, but the shifts have a cultural implication. On the surface it is a tale of academic emotional tangles. It is framed within the relationship between Benton, an English professor, and his friend and colleague Malcolm Totting, whose attempt to commit suicide begins the story and whose return from a long period rediscovering himself in Europe ends it. Totting's suicide attempt changes Benton's life, for after he has taken his friend to the hospital, he gets drunk and goes back to Totting's flat with one of his graduate students, a girl named Thalia. She becomes his mistress that night, and shortly afterwards his marriage breaks down, and he and Thalia with their child settle in the farmhouse he had rebuilt. Then there comes to the campus a visiting professor from Princeton, a woman with dyed blonde hair and a kind of lean, tanned hardness that at first makes Benton see her as a sexless symbol of the "heartland," of American and especially New York civilization. But slowly he becomes aware of Robyn's sexuality; they fall in love, or think they do — for so much of this story is about how academics live in their heads. They enjoy a brief affair, yet finally, because Benton cannot bear to hurt Thalia, they break apart. As the returning Totting laconically remarks, "Love is the worst."[60] Underlying the rather conventionally arranged love triangle, there is the level of cultural allegiances. Cohen seems to be hinting, though he states it in no obvious way, that for Canadians America is no escape. The successful journeys in *Café Le Dog* are not directed south of the border. They are to Europe, with its continuous history, its continuous culture; the journeys of the narrator's mother in "Café Le Dog" and of Joseph Benares in "Sentimental Meetings."

"Sentimental Meetings" is one of two stories whose links with *The Spanish Doctor* and the travels Cohen made in Europe as he researched the novel are very clear. The other is "The Sins of Tomas Benares." The protagonist of "Sentimental Meetings" is Tomas Benares' grandson Joseph. Long ago an ancestral Benares went, like Avram Halevi, from Spain to Kiev. Later some of the family return to Spain, which Tomas Benares — also, like Halevi, a Spanish doctor — leaves just before the civil war for Canada, where he has lived into old age. Tomas' "sins" are his sexual lapses, the most sensational being his night of exhausting passion at the age of seventy-four with his son's luscious widow, Bella. As the story ends, Tomas is ninety-four and Bella, who left after their night together, returns. Her continued vitality contrasts with his frailty and makes him aware of the nearness of Death, whom he defies in a gesture of celebrating his birthday through Bella's happy return. Durability is the theme of the story, which in its own way is a celebration of the Jewish people's power of survival in the endless journeying of the Diaspora.

Tomas does not return to Europe, but Joseph, his grandson and in his own way yet another "Spanish doctor," does, and in Paris he encounters a distant relative named Hanna Santangel, who had survived in the Europe of pogroms and holocausts. With Hanna he makes his journey back to Spain to close in the family's cycle of wandering, and there they find that the great synagogue that Samuel Halevi built in the fourteenth century is closed to Jewish visitors because a German film company is shooting there. The film, as the director explains when they finally do gain entry, is "a documentary on religious freedom . . . . I want to show that people are finally, after so much bloodshed, free to follow the god of their choice." "There is only one God," Hanna replies. "And people don't choose Him, He chooses them."[61] Yet it is the German director, ironically, who welcomes Joseph home as the Jew who has recognized his internationalism and so has found himself.

The perilous history of the Jewish people and its international destiny are exemplified in *The Spanish Doctor*, where Avram Halevi is endangered on the one hand because he is a Jew and on the other because he is a pioneer surgeon who risks his life performing illegal dissections and accumulating a vast knowledge of comparative anatomy; he believes, for a good part of his life, that with the science symbolized by his surgeon's knife he will "pare away superstition"[62] and bring about the reign of scientific light. Only half a Jew — bastard son of a Jewish woman raped by a Castilian soldier during a pogrom, forcibly converted to Christianity but not practising it — Avram is a man between two worlds, between Jew and gentile, between reason and faith.

After an opening flashback to Avram's violent origins, the real action begins with his return to Toledo, the town of his birth, from Montpellier, where he has perfected his skills as a surgeon. Shortly after his return, he is called to the house of a rich merchant, Juan Velásquez, and successfully performs a difficult caesarean on his wife, gaining in Don Juan an ambiguous friend and defender. These ties with the Velásquez family bring him into contact with Juan's brother, the Cardinal Rodrigo, who is filled with the passion to unite all Europe within the Christian religion and is prepared to exterminate the Jews in order to do so.

The cardinal leads a pogrom in which the Jewish quarter of Toledo is destroyed and its inhabitants are slaughtered, but Avram manages to flee back to Montpellier, which, though plague-stricken, is still to him the centre of medical research, the resting place of the scientific vision. His reputation as a doctor grows, and finally, forgetting his Toledo sweetheart Gabriela Hasdai, he marries into a family of Jews who have been converted into devout Catholics. Avram becomes dean of medicine at the University of Montpellier, and it seems as though his Jewishness is wiped out and his future in the world of prestige and power is assured.

But this is the uneasy Europe of the early fifteenth century, the time of the Great Schism, when rival popes reign in Avignon and Rome, and in the conflict within the Church the Jew becomes a ritual victim whom each side can persecute to prove the strength of its orthodoxy. A scandal rises over the blasphemies of one of Avram's students, and at the same time his most important Christian patron is disgraced. Avram finds that his nominal conversion is not enough to protect him. Cardinal Rodrigo arrives, drawn by the smell of heresy, and though Avram escapes once more and makes his way to Bologna, his wife kills herself, and their daughter is killed. Finally, in Bologna, the opportunity comes and Avram takes his revenge, assassinating the cardinal. He is captured, but he is kept alive because his survival proves the innocence of Rodrigo Velásquez's great enemy, the Cardinal Baldessare Cossa (the man who became Pope John XXIII and then was deposed in 1415 by the Council of Constance, which effectively reunited the Catholic church and ended the Great Schism). Avram eventually escapes and flees to Kiev, where he dies in peace and wisdom with his old love, Gabriela Hasdai.

The Spanish Doctor is a work of power and passion, but also of parody and palimpsest, for it involves us deeply in the problems of historical fiction in our generation. In a way, all history is palimpsest. No historian presents the past exactly as it was, partly because historians cannot know it all, and partly because what they do know is so formless that, if they did not reshape it and write it to their conjectures, it would be incomprehensible. Historical novelists carry the process farther than historians by melding the facts of history into an invented course of action, and some of them add a philosophic intent. In such novels, there is often a tendency to defy the plausible in the process of reshaping events to fit a didactic or aesthetic structure. And here the modern novelists who turn to historical fiction are inclined, as Matt Cohen is in *The Spanish Doctor*, to seem arbitrary in their combination of actual and invented history, and to use methods that lead us to question the possibility of a literal reconstruction of the past.

The whole structure of the narrative in *The Spanish Doctor* is in fact an elaborate palimpsest. The real history of the persecution of Jews in fifteenth-century Europe is overlaid by the search of Avram

Halevi, the pioneer doctor, for the liberation that will come from the recognition of scientific truth, enlivened by violent action that is a deliberate parody of the swashbuckling novel in the manner of Alexandre Dumas. Avram's achievement of a kind of sanctity in distant exile, his character forged by suffering and annealed by misfortune, is a further writing over, a symbolic vindication of a universal humanity that cannot be imposed from outside, at the hands of murdering fanatics such as Rodrigo Velásquez and his twentieth-century successors, but only learned by each man himself, through outer experience and inner recognition.

The Spanish Doctor, in spite of its rich impasto of garnered and researched detail, is as implausible and yet as ultimately true as *The Sweet Second Summer of Kitty Malone*.

NOTES

[1] Letter received from Matt Cohen (1983).

[2] Alan Twigg, "Matt Cohen: Eastern Horizon," in *For Openers: Conversations with Twenty-Four Canadian Writers* (Madeira Park, B.C.: Harbour, 1981), p. 181. All further references to this work (Twigg) appear in the text.

[3] George Orwell, "Why I Write," in *An Age Like This: 1920–1940*, Vol. 1 of *The Collected Essays, Journalism and Letters of George Orwell*, ed. Sonia Orwell and Ian Angus (New York: Harcourt, Brace & World, 1968), p. 7.

[4] Wayne R. Smith, "Novel about Rise of Pop Singer Spoiled by Incoherent Writing," rev. of *Johnny Crackle Sings*, *The Citizen* [Ottawa], 24 Dec. 1971, p. 33.

[5] Doug Austen, "Johnny Crackle," rev. of *Johnny Crackle Sings*, *Guerilla* [Toronto], 24 Nov. 1971, p. 17.

[6] Donald Cameron, "The Musings of a Literary Beachcomber," rev. of *Johnny Crackle Sings*, and nine other books, *Maclean's*, Feb. 1972, p. 88.

[7] Jack Batten, "Real Chips off the Rock," rev. of *Johnny Crackle Sings*, *The Globe Magazine*, 9 Oct. 1971, p. 19.

[8] Douglas Barbour, "New Freedoms in Canadian Fiction," rev. of *72: New Canadian Stories*, ed. David Helwig and Joan Harcourt, *Noman*, by Gwendolyn MacEwen, and *Columbus and the Fat Lady and Other Stories*, by Matt Cohen, *Edmonton Journal*, 9 Feb. 1973, p. Tab 5.

[9] Robert Harlow, "Confections beyond Our Booksellers," rev. of *The*

Story of a Cat, by John Newlove, and *Columbus and the Fat Lady and Other Stories*, by Matt Cohen, *Maclean's*, March 1973, p. 96.

[10] Wilma Breakwell, "New Book 'Dreary' in Brilliant Prose," rev. of *The Disinherited*, *The Owen Sound Sun-Times*, 18 April 1974, p. 6.

[11] David Watmough, rev. of *The Disinherited*, CBC Radio [1974].

[12] David McFadden, "A Canadian Novel Built to Last," rev. of *The Disinherited*, *The Spectator* [Hamilton], 23 March 1974, p. 4.

[13] Jack Batten, "Masterful. As Real as That Ugly Lady with Her Mustache," rev. of *The Disinherited*, *The Globe and Mail*, 23 March 1974, p. 32.

[14] Patricia Morley, "Courage, Comedy and Seeking Eden," rev. of *The Disinherited*, *Ottawa Journal*, 28 Sept. 1974, p. 40.

[15] Roy MacSkimming, "Gothic Tales in the Country of Defeat," rev. of *The Disinherited*, *Saturday Night*, May 1974, p. 42.

[16] Anthony Brennan, "The Nomads of Ontario," rev. of *The Disinherited*, *The Fiddlehead*, No. 102 (Summer 1974), p. 112.

[17] John Moss, Introd., *The Disinherited*, New Canadian Library, No. 121 (Toronto: McClelland and Stewart, 1976), p. xii.

[18] John Mills, rev. of *The Hungry Hills*, by George Ryga, and *Wooden Hunters*, by Matt Cohen, *The Fiddlehead*, No. 107 (Fall 1975), pp. 135, 136.

[19] Paul Stuewe, "The Novel as Shadows," rev. of *Wooden Hunters*, *Books in Canada*, April 1975, p. 8.

[20] Francis Mansbridge, rev. of *Wooden Hunters*, *Canadian Fiction Magazine*, No. 20 (Winter 1976), p. 102.

[21] George Russell, "Message of Despair," rev. of *Wooden Hunters*, *Time* [Canadian ed.], 19 May 1975, p. 16.

[22] John Ayre, "Matt Cohen's View: Blood, Impotence and Absurdity," rev. of *Wooden Hunters*, *Saturday Night*, May 1975, p. 70.

[23] Roy MacSkimming, "Gifted Novelist Makes Characters Hard to Forget," rev. of *Wooden Hunters*, *The Toronto Star*, 15 March 1975, Sec. D, p. 9.

[24] Jack Batten, "Cohen Will Make You Care," rev. of *Wooden Hunters*, *The Globe and Mail*, 15 March 1975, p. 31.

[25] Norman Snider, "No Apocalypse — Just a Sneeze. Armies Marching in the Night? Now Really!" rev. of *The Colours of War*, *The Globe and Mail*, 20 Aug. 1977, p. 34.

[26] Tom Middlebro', "Nightmare without Motives," rev. of *The Colours of War*, *The Citizen* [Ottawa], 8 Oct. 1977, p. 34.

[27] Peter Stevens, "A Canadian Parable, Perhaps," rev. of *The Colours of War*, *The Windsor Star*, 29 Oct. 1977, p. 51. In Stevens' review, the names of

Theodore and his father, Jacob, are mistakenly reversed. The corrected name appears in square brackets.

[28] Ken Adachi, "Flawed Novel of Canada at War Stretches Belief," rev. of *The Colours of War*, *The Toronto Star*, 3 Sept. 1977, Sec. G, p. 7.

[29] Timothy Findley, rev. of *The Sweet Second Summer of Kitty Malone*, *The Globe and Mail*, 3 March 1979, p. 44.

[30] Gerald Noonan, "Matt Cohen's Novel Is a Triumph," rev. of *The Sweet Second Summer of Kitty Malone*, *The Toronto Star*, 24 Feb. 1979, Sec. D, p. 7.

[31] Patricia Morley, "Personal Past Alive in Present," rev. of *The Sweet Second Summer of Kitty Malone*, *Ottawa Journal*, 3 March 1979, p. 51.

[32] Barbara Amiel, "Secrets Not Yet Whispered," rev. of *The Sweet Second Summer of Kitty Malone*, *Maclean's*, 12 March 1979, p. 54.

[33] Michael Thorpe, "High on Obsessions," rev. of *Night Flights: Stories New and Selected*, *Books in Canada*, May 1978, p. 16.

[34] Jon Kertzer, "Delusion and Reality," rev. of *Night Flights: Stories New and Selected*, *The Canadian Forum*, June–July 1978, pp. 48, 49.

[35] Gary T. Davenport, "A Canadian Miscellany," rev. of *Toronto Short Stories*, ed. Morris Wolfe and Douglas Daymond, *The Wars*, by Timothy Findley, and *Night Flights: Stories New and Selected*, by Matt Cohen, *The Sewanee Review*, 87 (Winter 1979), xxi.

[36] Ken Adachi, "Hatred and Lust on the Farm," rev. of *Flowers of Darkness*, *The Toronto Star*, 21 Feb. 1981, Sec. F, p. 10.

[37] Douglas Hamilton, "'Flowers' Blooms with Dark Irony," rev. of *Flowers of Darkness*, *The Toronto Star*, 11 April 1981, p. 60.

[38] Wayne Grady, "Cohen's Chronicles," rev. of *Flowers of Darkness*, *Saturday Night*, March 1981, pp. 50, 51.

[39] George Woodcock, "Shady Leaves of Destiny," rev. of *Flowers of Darkness*, *Books in Canada*, March 1981, p. 12.

[40] Paul Stuewe, "Pastoral Peccadillos and Parochial Passion," rev. of *Flowers of Darkness*, *Quill & Quire*, Feb. 1981, p. 45.

[41] Aritha van Herk, "Salem Lives in Cohen's Darkest Canada," rev. of *Flowers of Darkness*, *The Vancouver Sun*, 3 April 1981, Sec. L, p. 35.

[42] Anthony Bukoski, "Dead Souls," rev. of *Café Le Dog*, *Books in Canada*, Nov. 1983, pp. 29, 30.

[43] George Galt, "The Hollow Men," rev. of *Café Le Dog*, *Saturday Night*, Nov. 1983, p. 76.

[44] Ken Adachi, "Matt Cohen's Short Stories Leave Reviewer Longing for His Novels," rev. of *Café Le Dog*, *The Toronto Star*, 5 Nov. 1983, Sec. F, p. 10.

[45] William French, "Some Abbreviated Lessons in Love from Matt Cohen," rev. of *Café Le Dog*, *The Globe and Mail*, 20 Oct. 1983, Sec. E, p. 1.

[46] Jon Kertzer, "The Violence of Passion," rev. of *Café Le Dog*, *The Canadian Forum*, Nov. 1983, pp. 34, 35.

[47] Mark Abley, "A Distant Fictional Mirror," rev. of *The Spanish Doctor, Maclean's*, 17 Sept. 1984, p. 68h.

[48] Alberto Manguel, "The Spanish Doctor: Stranger in His Own Land," *Quill & Quire*, Aug. 1984, p. 29.

[49] Norman Sigurdson, "A Huge Literary Anachronism," rev. of *The Spanish Doctor, Winnipeg Free Press*, 22 Sept. 1984, p. 50.

[50] Ken Adachi, "A Brave Venture Brings with It Very Little Magic," rev. of *The Spanish Doctor, The Toronto Star*, 15 Sept. 1984, Sec. M, p. 4.

[51] Frank Davey, "Persistent Dilemmas," rev. of *The Spanish Doctor*, *The Canadian Forum*, Jan. 1985, p. 37.

[52] *Night Flights: Stories New and Selected* (Toronto: Doubleday, 1978), p. 14. All further references to this work (*NF*) appear in the text.

[53] *Korsoniloff* (Toronto: House of Anansi, 1969), p. 42. All further references to this work appear in the text.

[54] *The Disinherited* (Toronto: McClelland and Stewart, 1974), pp. 145–46. All further references to this work appear in the text.

[55] *Wooden Hunters* (Toronto: McClelland and Stewart, 1975), p. 14. All further references to this work appear in the text.

[56] *The Colours of War* (Toronto: McClelland and Stewart, 1977), pp. 16–17. All further references to this work appear in the text.

[57] *The Sweet Second Summer of Kitty Malone* (Toronto: McClelland and Stewart, 1979), pp. 158–59. All further references to this work appear in the text.

[58] *Flowers of Darkness* (Toronto: McClelland and Stewart, 1981), pp. 58–59. All further references to this work appear in the text.

[59] Matt Cohen, "Notes on Realism in Modern English-Canadian Fiction," *Canadian Literature*, No. 100 (Spring 1984), p. 70.

[60] "Golden Whore of the Heartland," in *Café Le Dog* (Toronto: McClelland and Stewart, 1983), p. 60.

[61] "Sentimental Meetings," in *Café Le Dog*, p. 123.

[62] *The Spanish Doctor* (Toronto: McClelland and Stewart, 1984), p. 29.

SELECTED BIBLIOGRAPHY

Primary Sources

Cohen, Matt. "Albert Camus's Political Thought." M.A. Thesis Toronto 1965.
———. *Korsoniloff*. Toronto: House of Anansi, 1969.
———. *Johnny Crackle Sings*. Toronto: McClelland and Stewart, 1971.
———. *Columbus and the Fat Lady and Other Stories*. Toronto: House of Anansi, 1972.
———. *Too Bad Galahad*. Toronto: Coach House, 1972.
———, ed. *The Story So Far 2*. Toronto: Coach House, 1973.
———. *The Disinherited*. Toronto: McClelland and Stewart, 1974.
———. *Peach Melba*. Toronto: Coach House, 1974.
———. *Wooden Hunters*. Toronto: McClelland and Stewart, 1975.
———. *The Colours of War*. Toronto: McClelland and Stewart, 1977.
———. *The Leaves of Louise*. Toronto: McClelland and Stewart, 1978.
———. *Night Flights: Stories New and Selected*. Toronto: Doubleday, 1978.
———. *The Sweet Second Summer of Kitty Malone*. Toronto: McClelland and Stewart, 1979.
———. *Flowers of Darkness*. Toronto: McClelland and Stewart, 1981.
———. *The Expatriate: Collected Short Stories*. New Press Canadian Classics. Toronto: General, 1982.
———. *Café Le Dog*. Toronto: McClelland and Stewart, 1983.
———. "Notes on Realism in Modern English-Canadian Fiction." *Canadian Literature*, No. 100 (Spring 1984), pp. 65–71.
———. *The Spanish Doctor*. Toronto: McClelland and Stewart, 1984.

Secondary Sources

Abley, Mark. "A Distant Fictional Mirror." Rev. of *The Spanish Doctor*. *Maclean's*, 17 Sept. 1984, p. 68h.

Adachi, Ken. "Flawed Novel of Canada at War Stretches Belief." Rev. of *The Colours of War*. *The Toronto Star*, 3 Sept. 1977, Sec. G, p. 7.

———. "Hatred and Lust Down on the Farm." Rev. of *Flowers of Darkness*. *The Toronto Star*, 21 Feb. 1981, Sec. F, p. 10.

———. "Matt Cohen's Short Stories Leave Reviewer Longing for His Novels." Rev. of *Café Le Dog*. *The Toronto Star*, 5 Nov. 1983, Sec. F, p. 10.

———. "A Brave Venture Brings with It Very Little Magic." Rev. of *The Spanish Doctor*. *The Toronto Star*, 15 Sept. 1984, Sec. M, p. 4.

Amiel, Barbara. "Secrets Not Yet Whispered." Rev. of *The Sweet Second Summer of Kitty Malone*. *Maclean's*, 12 March 1979, p. 54.

Austen, Doug. "Johnny Crackle." Rev. of *Johnny Crackle Sings*. *Guerilla* [Toronto], 24 Nov. 1971, p. 17.

Ayre, John. "Matt Cohen's View: Blood, Impotence and Absurdity." Rev. of *Wooden Hunters*. *Saturday Night*, May 1975, pp. 69–70.

Barbour, Douglas. "New Freedom in Canadian Fiction." Rev. of *72: New Canadian Stories*, ed. David Helwig and Joan Harcourt, *Noman*, by Gwendolyn MacEwen, and *Columbus and the Fat Lady and Other Stories*, by Matt Cohen. *Edmonton Journal*, 9 Feb. 1973, p. Tab 5.

Batten, Jack. "Real Chips off the Rock." Rev. of *Johnny Crackle Sings*. *The Globe Magazine*, 9 Oct. 1971, p. 19.

———. "Masterful. As Real as That Ugly Lady with Her Mustache." Rev. of *The Disinherited*. *The Globe and Mail*, 23 March 1974, p. 32.

———. "Cohen Will Make You Care." Rev. of *Wooden Hunters*. *The Globe and Mail*, 15 March 1975, p. 31.

Breakwell, Wilma. "New Book 'Dreary' in Brilliant Prose." Rev. of *The Disinherited*. *The Owen Sound Sun-Times*, 18 April 1974, p. 6.

Brennan, Anthony. "The Nomads of Ontario." Rev. of *The Disinherited*. *The Fiddlehead*, No. 102 (Summer 1974), pp. 107–12.

Bukoski, Anthony. "Dead Souls." Rev. of *Café Le Dog*. *Books in Canada*, Nov. 1983, pp. 29–30.

Cameron, Donald. "The Musings of a Literary Beachcomber." Rev. of *Johnny Crackle Sings*, and nine other books. *Maclean's*, Feb. 1972, p. 88.

Davenport, Gary T. "A Canadian Miscellany." Rev. of *Toronto Short Stories*, ed. Morris Wolfe and Douglas Daymond, *The Wars*, by Timothy Findley, and *Night Flights: Stories New and Selected*, by Matt Cohen. *The Sewanee Review*, 87 (Winter 1979), xix-xxii.

Davey, Frank. "Matt Cohen." In *From There to Here: A Guide to English-Canadian Literature since 1960*. Erin, Ont.: Porcépic, 1974, pp. 73–77.

———. "Persistent Dilemmas." Rev. of *The Spanish Doctor*. *The Canadian Forum*, Jan. 1985, pp. 36–37.

Findley, Timothy. Rev. of *The Sweet Second Summer of Kitty Malone*. *The Globe and Mail*, 3 March 1979, p. 44.

French, William. "Some Abbreviated Lessons in Love from Matt Cohen." Rev. of *Café Le Dog*. *The Globe and Mail*, 20 Oct. 1983, Sec. E, p. 1.

Galt, George. "The Hollow Men." Rev. of *Café Le Dog*. *Saturday Night*, Nov. 1983, p. 76.

Gibson, Graeme. "Matt Cohen." In *Eleven Canadian Novelists Interviewed by Graeme Gibson*. Toronto: House of Anansi, 1973, pp. 59–84.

Grady, Wayne. "Cohen's Chronicle." Rev. of *Flowers of Darkness*. *Saturday Night*, March 1981, pp. 50–51.

Hamilton, Douglas. "'Flowers' Blooms with Dark Irony." Rev. of *Flowers of Darkness*. *The Toronto Star*, 11 April 1981, p. 60.

Harlow, Robert. "Confections beyond Our Booksellers." Rev. of *The Story of a Cat*, by John Newlove, and *Columbus and the Fat Lady and Other Stories*, by Matt Cohen. *Maclean's*, March 1973, p. 96.

Kertzer, Jon. "Delusion and Reality." Rev. of *Night Flights: Stories New and Selected*. *The Canadian Forum*, June–July 1978, pp. 48–49.

———. "The Violence of Passion." Rev. of *Café Le Dog*. *The Canadian Forum*, Nov. 1983, pp. 34–35.

MacSkimming, Roy. "Gothic Tales in the Country of Defeat." Rev. of *The Disinherited*. *Saturday Night*, May 1974, pp. 41–42.

———. "Gifted Novelist Makes Characters Hard to Forget." Rev. of *Wooden Hunters*. *The Toronto Star*, 15 March 1975, Sec. D, p. 9.

Manguel, Alberto. "The Spanish Doctor: Stranger in His Own Land." *Quill & Quire*, Aug. 1984, p. 29.

Mansbridge, Francis. Rev. of *Wooden Hunters*. *Canadian Fiction Magazine*, No. 20 (Winter 1976), pp. 101–02.

McFadden, David. "A Canadian Novel Built to Last." Rev. of *The Disinherited*. *The Spectator* [Hamilton], 23 March 1974, p. 4.

Middlebro', Tom. "Nightmare without Motives." Rev. of *The Colours of War*. *The Citizen* [Ottawa], 8 Oct. 1977, p. 34.

Mills, John. Rev. of *The Hungry Hills*, by George Ryga, and *Wooden Hunters*, by Matt Cohen. *The Fiddlehead*, No. 107 (Fall 1975), pp. 133–36.

Morley, Patricia. "Courage, Comedy and Seeking Eden." Rev. of *The Disinherited*. *Ottawa Journal*, 28 Sept. 1974, p. 40.

———. "Personal Past Alive in Present." Rev. of *The Sweet Second Summer of Kitty Malone*. *Ottawa Journal*, 3 March 1979, p. 51.

Moss, John, introd. *Wooden Hunters*. New Canadian Library, No. 149. Toronto: McClelland and Stewart, 1975, pp. v–xii.

———, introd. *The Disinherited*. New Canadian Library, No. 121.

Toronto: McClelland and Stewart, 1976, pp. vii–xiii.

Noonan, Gerald. "Matt Cohen's Novel Is a Triumph." Rev. of *The Sweet Second Summer of Kitty Malone*. *The Toronto Star*, 24 Feb. 1979, p. D7.

Orwell, George. "Why I Write." In *An Age Like This: 1920–1940*. Vol. 1 of *The Collected Essays, Journalism and Letters of George Orwell*. Ed. Sonia Orwell and Ian Angus. New York: Harcourt, Brace & World, 1968, pp. 1–7.

Russell, George. "Message of Despair." Rev. of *Wooden Hunters*. *Time* [Canadian ed.], 19 May 1975, p. 16.

Sigurdson, Norman. "A Huge Literary Anachronism." Rev. of *The Spanish Doctor*. *Winnipeg Free Press*, 22 Sept. 1984, p. 50.

Smith, Wayne R. "Novel about Rise of Pop Singer Spoiled by Incoherent Writing." Rev. of *Johnny Crackle Sings*. *The Citizen* [Ottawa], 24 Dec. 1971, p. 33.

Snider, Norman. "No Apocalypse — Just a Sneeze. Armies Marching in the Night? Now Really!" Rev. of *The Colours of War*. *The Globe and Mail*, 20 Aug. 1977, p. 34.

Stevens, Peter. "A Canadian Parable, Perhaps." Rev. of *The Colours of War*. *The Windsor Star*, 29 Oct. 1977, p. 51.

Story, Norah. "Matt Cohen." In *Supplement to the Oxford Companion to Canadian History and Literature*. Ed. William Toye. Toronto: Oxford Univ. Press, 1973, pp. 45–46.

Stuewe, Paul. "The Novel as Shadows." Rev. of *Wooden Hunters*. *Books in Canada*, April 1975, pp. 8–9.

———. "Pastoral Peccadillos and Parochial Passion." Rev. of *Flowers of Darkness*. *Quill & Quire*, Feb. 1981, p. 45.

Thorpe, Michael. "High on Obsessions." Rev. of *Night Flights: Stories New and Selected*. *Books in Canada*, May 1978, pp. 15–16.

Twigg, Alan. "Matt Cohen: Eastern Horizon." In *For Openers: Conversations with Twenty-Four Canadian Writers*. Madeira Park, B.C.: Harbour, 1981, pp. 175–84.

van Herk, Aritha. "Salem Lives in Cohen's Darkest Canada." Rev. of *Flowers of Darkness*. *The Vancouver Sun*, 3 April 1981, Sec. L, p. 35.

Watmough, David. Rev. of *The Disinherited*. CBC Radio [1974].

Woodcock, George. "Five New Novelists Enter the Literary Lottery." Rev. of *Korsoniloff*, and four other books. *Toronto Daily Star*, 11 Oct. 1969, p. 25.

———. "To the Past via the Future." Rev. of *The Colours of War*. *Canadian Literature*, No. 75 (Winter 1977), pp. 74–77.

———. "Armies Moving in the Night: The Fictions of Matt Cohen." *Inter-*

national Fiction Review, 6, No. 1 (Winter 1979), 17–30. Rpt. (rev.) in *The World of Canadian Writing: Critiques and Recollections*. Vancouver: Douglas & McIntyre, 1980, pp. 127–48.

———. "Matt Cohen's Loyalist Kingdom." Rev. of *The Sweet Second Summer of Kitty Malone*. *Saturday Night*, April 1979, pp. 67–68.

———. "Shady Leaves of Destiny." Rev. of *Flowers of Darkness*. *Books in Canada*, March 1981, pp. 11–12.